I wish I had read ⟨...⟩ ⟨...⟩ ⟨...⟩ ⟨...⟩ /arent. In this book, Michael Kennedy offers realistic and hopeful counsel for parents on raising children grounded in the gospel. Thought-provoking questions, healthy biblical teaching, and pertinent cultural awareness make this book a vital resource for parents today. If you care about the next generation, read this!

Dr. Alvin L. Reid, Professor of Evangelism and Student
Ministry/Bailey Smith Chair of Evangelism
Southeastern Baptist Theological Seminary
Pastor to Young Professionals,
Richland Creek Community Church, Wake Forest, NC

Parent-Driven Discipleship is a timely and much-needed work. In a day in which the idea of parenting and the idea of discipleship is grossly misunderstood we need clarity and biblical substance to bring us back to a right understanding. Michael Kennedy's book does just that. It is well written, accessible, and will be a great help to parents seeking to honor God and raise their children rightly. Highly recommended!

Dr. Wyman Richardson, Senior Pastor
Central Baptist Church
North Little Rock, AR

Parent-Driven Discipleship presents a message that every church and parent needs to hear, making disciples begins in the home. Through biblically based teaching and practical application, Michael presents steps that parents and children can take together to follow after the Lord Jesus Christ. As an added bonus, the personal questionnaires allow the reader to interact with the material through self-assessment and reflection. *Parent-Driven Discipleship* offers those who dare to fully engage an opportunity to make a difference in the lives of their children and their churches.

Dr. Rusty Ricketson,
Professor of Leadership
Luther Rice Seminary and University
Lithonia, GA

The mind of a scholar and the heart of a father come together to unveil the essentials to great parenting in *Parent-Driven Discipleship*.

Jason Waters, Student Pastor,
First Baptist Church
Norfolk, VA

When I am looking for resources to help disciple parents and families, I am always looking for a resource that is practical and will be helpful for anyone that picks it up. I know that the families that pass through the door of my church building on Sunday morning come from all walks of life and I need to be ready to engage them with resources to help them be godly parents that raise the next godly generation. *Parent-Driven Discipleship* is going to be one of those tools that I quickly put in their hands.

Here are three reasons why I am sold on this book. 1) It is probing. This book easily leads the reader to critically think about where they are and where they need to be as parents. 2) It is practical. The reader is guided to take the biblical priority of parent driven discipleship with achievable steps that will build confidence in any mom or dad. 3) It is powerful. While biblically sound, it isn't too deep to fly over the reader's head, yet it challenges them enough to long to be a godly parent. God's Word is intertwined throughout this book and the basis for Michael's instruction rests on the Bible. God desires that Christian parents raise godly young men and women. I believe that *Parent-Driven Discipleship* will help us equip our church leaders and families to watch it come to fruition.

Chris Young, Teaching and Family Pastor,
Central Baptist Church
Warner Robins, GA

PARENT-DRIVEN DISCIPLESHIP

MICHAEL KENNEDY

Energion Publications
Gonzalez, FL
2015

Cover Image Credit:
© Anthonycz | Dreamstime.com - Drawing Of Family Photo

ISBN10: 1-63199-149-3
ISBN13: 978-1-63199-149-3
Library of Congress Control Number: 2015950359

Energion Publications
P. O. Box 841
Gonzalez, FL 32560
energion.com
pubs@energion.com
850-525-3916

For my wife, Janie,
and our girls, Anna and Leah

TABLE OF CONTENTS

FOREWORD

The deterioration of the traditional family has been well documented and the evidence of its demise casts an ominous shadow on our churches and communities. The erosion of the nuclear family is not only chronicled in research journals but is also obvious through shifting cultural norms that are establishing a new "modern family." But even contemporary attempts to redefine the family provide evidence of its foundational importance. Cultures and communities cannot be established apart from families, no matter how they are defined.

While we would like to throw stones from a safe distance at the culture's attempt to distort the traditional family, the Church has become guilty of the same crime but with different weapons. Instead of murdering the sacred institution of marriage, we have, in many ways, abdicated our responsibilities as parents by spiritually abandoning our children. We have, in essence, converted the church into a spiritual orphanage where we enlist other people to spiritually raise our children.

While their growth must occur within true spiritual community, and there are occasions where the church is the only spiritual family some children have, the immediate family is God's designed and intended nest for nurturing. Parents are entrusted with the primary and fundamental responsibility that cannot be relinquished to a spiritual surrogate – the discipleship of their children.

This enormous responsibility that parents bear is established on a multi-layered basis. Theologically, we can recognize it through the paternal love and discipline that our heavenly Father faithfully demonstrates towards us (Hebrews 12:5-11). Biblically, we can see it in the imperative instructions given to parents (Ephesians 6:1-2, Deuteronomy 6:4-9). Ministerially, Paul uses parents, the mother and the father, as the metaphorical models for loving service, guidance, and leadership (1 Thessalonians 2:7-8, 11-12).

Each of these layers reinforces the accountability we have before God for the spiritual development of our children. But acknowledging the responsibility does not guarantee the remedy. The issue is as much of a pragmatic one as it is a diagnostic one. Ultimately, parents may embrace their primary role in discipleship but not know "where to begin or how to proceed."

This phrase exemplifies why *Parent-Driven Discipleship* is such a valuable resource. In this concise and insightful book Michael Kennedy offers a compelling case and useful guide for parents to take the spiritual reins of their family and disciple their children the way the Lord intended. It is thoroughly biblical and extremely practical. It is not only informative; it is instructional.

This descriptive phrase would also be an appropriate characterization of Michael and myself when we first met. I was a student pastor with a young family and he was a recently married seminary student who was eager to make a difference. Somehow, through hours of personal and prayerful conversations, we formulated some plans, invested in students, and watched the Lord do some amazing things that we still marvel at today.

Now, over a decade later, God continues to burden our hearts and clarify our vision for how to reach this next generation. As parents ourselves, we now sense an even greater burden to see our own children walking in the truth. We have come to realize, and continue to learn, that ultimately the responsibility for our children's spiritual growth must begin with us.

This book is a result of Michael's deep conviction of this truth. His passion for young people and their families encouraged me in our early years serving together and it continues to inspire me today. I know it will do the same for you as you consume and digest *Parent-Driven Discipleship*.

In His grace,
R. Scott Pace, Ph.D.
Reverend A. E. and Dora Johnson Hughes
Chair of Christian Ministry,
Oklahoma Baptist University

INTRODUCTION

A JOURNEY BEGINS

I remember it like it was yesterday. My wife looked at me with great excitement and said the greatest words a husband can hear, "Honey, I'm pregnant." There is no doubt I felt a thousand different emotions at that point in time – joy, thanksgiving, excitement, anxiousness, and, in all reality, fear. Questions began to pop up in my mind. Was I ready to be a father? Did I have what it takes to raise a child? What kind of father would I be? Would my child love Jesus? I was a father in the strict sense of the word but was I ready to be a real father, a godly father? This thought gripped me. I heard the words of former professors and pastors reverberating in my mind:

> "Parents are held accountable to teach their children the truths of God's Word."

> "It is your responsibility, as a parent, to live a life that displays the saving gospel of Jesus Christ to your children."

No. That was my answer. I was not prepared to handle this sort of responsibility. This is not the answer I had hoped to come up with. I wanted to be able to stick out my chest with confidence and assurance and claim, "I am the man for the job." After all, I was about to graduate from seminary. I had taken Bible classes and theology classes. I could parse Greek verbs and discuss the complexities of the Trinity. If anyone should have been prepared, it would have been me. The problem was I knew I was not the man for the job – at least not yet. This realization drove me to study God's Word and seek to understand better my responsibility. I wanted to know what God expected of me. I wanted to know how people, throughout church history, had taught their children the truths of Scripture. I wanted my child to love and serve Jesus and I knew I would play a huge role in his or her life.

When Jesus left this earth he gave his disciples a mission. This mission, also known as the Great Commission, is to make disciples of all nations, baptize them, and teach them to observe all of Jesus' commandments. What a daunting task! Much of the world was hostile to Christianity at this point in time and yet, this was the singular mission Jesus gave His disciples. In fact, the Great Commission was so important that the Holy Spirit guided every gospel writer to include it in their gospel accounts and Luke also included it in the book of Acts (Matthew 28:16-20, Mark 16:14-18, Luke 24:44-49, John 20:19-23, Acts 1:4-8). If we are to understand our role, with respect to our children, we must begin with the Great Commission. The mission of every believer is to make disciples and I can think of no better place to begin than with our own children. Parents should be disciple-makers, first and foremost, in the home.

I am always fascinated by new technology and one of the newest technologies on the market is the ability for cars to parallel park themselves. As the driver, you simply push a button, take your hands off the wheel, and allow the computer to guide the car into the parking place. This technology is amazing and works well but my fear is that we have taken the same approach to the spiritual development of our children. Often, we expect to be able to push a button, take our hands off the wheel, and our children will magically become the spiritual giants that we hoped they would become.

Statistics reveal that Christian parents are rarely involved in the spiritual lives of their children. Scripture, however, paints a very different picture of what this relationship should look like. As parents, we have the responsibility to "drive" the discipleship process in the home. We must keep our hands on the wheel and take responsibility to guide our children as they journey through life. This includes purposefully sharing the gospel with them, teaching them the ways of the Lord, and modeling for them a Great Commission focused lifestyle. The purpose of this book is to examine the biblical responsibility parents have to be involved in their children's spiritual lives and help equip them to take an active role.

The end goal of this book is that parents and churches will renew their efforts to train this generation of children and teenagers. My greatest desire is that this generation will know Jesus and make Him known throughout the world.

FULL-SCALE ASSAULT: DECLARING WAR ON THE FAMILY

Did you know you are at war? This very moment you are being attacked and you may not even know. Ever since Satan deceived Adam and Eve in the garden, he has continually launched a full-scale assault on marriage and the family. Dr. James Dobson, in his book *Marriage Under Fire*, wrote,

> To put it succinctly, the institution of marriage represents the very foundation of human social order. Everything of value sits on that base. Institutions, governments, religious fervor, and the welfare of children are all dependent on its stability. When it is weakened or undermined, the entire superstructure begins to wobble. That is exactly what has happened during the last thirty-five years, as radical feminists, liberal lawmakers, and profiteers in the entertainment industry have taken their toll on the stability of marriage. Many of our pressing social problems can be traced to this origin.[1]

---

1   James Dobson, *Marriage Under Fire* (Colorado Springs, CO: Multnoma Publishers, 2004), 4

Satan is no dummy. He knows that strong Christian families are a detriment to his plans and purposes on this earth and he is doing everything possible to destroy every one of them, including yours. My desire is not to scare you but to sound the alarm. We must open our eyes to reality. In this chapter, we are going to spend some time exploring the origins of the family and the havoc that Satan can bring into the life of the family. We are also going to take a look at the culture around us so that we can see first hand how he is trying to accomplish his mission.

THE FAMILY BEGINS

Are you skeptical of institutions? Many people are and the reason is quite clear – they do not trust institutions. In fact, we have all seen institutions fail because of corruption (think Enron). I want you to consider something that may cause you to think about institutions a little differently. Did you know the very first institution that God created was the family? Yes, that's right – the very first institution ever created by God was the family. Consider these verses,

> *Then God said, "Let us make man in our image, after our likeness. And let them have dominion over the fish of the sea and over the birds of the heavens and over the livestock and over all the earth and over every creeping thing that creeps on the earth." So God created man in his own image, in the image of God he created him; male and female he created them. And God blessed them. And God said to them, "Be fruitful and multiply and fill the earth and subdue it, and have dominion over the fish of the sea and over the birds of the heavens and over every living thing that moves on the earth." And God said, "Behold, I have given you every plant yielding seed that is on the face of all the earth, and every tree with seed in its fruit. You shall have them for food. And to every beast of the earth and to every bird of the heavens and to everything that creeps on the earth, everything that has the breath of life, I have given every green plant for food." And it was so. And God saw everything that he had made, and behold,*

it was very good. And there was evening and there was morning, the sixth day.[2]

After God had created everything else, he crafted his most glorious creation: man and woman. Mankind is the only creature that is made in the image of God. We are special. We are unique.

After God created Adam and Eve, he brought them together and performed the very first wedding in history. He then gave them two primary responsibilities: (1) "be fruitful and multiply and fill the earth" and (2) "subdue it and have dominion over the fish of the sea and over the birds of the heavens and over every living thing that moves on the earth." Essentially, these two commands can be summed up in two words: procreate and steward. Adam and Eve were called to fill the earth with true worshipers of God and steward all of God's other creation. The plan was simple and yet, very quickly, things began to unravel.

Satan Declares War

Satan is a rebel. He enjoyed the privilege of being in the presence of the Lord but chose to lead a rebellion in heaven. As a result, he was banished from God's presence (along with 1/3 of the angels) and cast down to the earth. You would think that this severe rebuke and punishment would have been devastating to Satan. Yet, the reality is that it stoked the fires of his prideful rebellion and he sought to bring God's rule and reign to dust. That is where we come into the picture. Consider the story as recorded in Genesis 3:1-7:

> *Now the serpent was more crafty than any other beast of the field that the LORD God had made. He said to the woman, "Did God actually say, 'You shall not eat of any tree in the garden'?" And the woman said to the serpent, "We may eat of the fruit of the trees in the garden, but God said, 'You shall not eat of the fruit of the tree that is in the midst of the garden, neither shall you touch it, lest you die.'" But the serpent said to the woman, "You will not surely die. For God knows that when you eat of it your eyes will be opened, and you will be like God, knowing good and evil." So*

---

2   Genesis 1:26-31

when the woman saw that the tree was good for food, and that it was a delight to the eyes, and that the tree was to be desired to make one wise, she took of its fruit and ate, and she also gave some to her husband who was with her, and he ate.

Adam and Eve (the very first human beings) enjoyed God's presence in the garden and had full reign over all the rest of creation. God had only given them one "no, no" – they were not to eat of the tree of the knowledge of good and evil (Genesis 2:16-17). They could eat from every other tree in the garden but this one, specific tree was off limits. The punishment for eating the fruit of this tree would be death (spiritual and physical).

Satan was not content with being the only rebel; he wanted other rebels – people who would throw off God's rule and reign in their lives. Adam and Eve were perfect targets. Satan was crafty, craftier than any other beast that God had created. He appeared to Eve as a snake and unfolded his grand plan of rebellion. He did not call it a plan of rebellion but that is exactly what it turned out to be. Satan deceived Eve and caused her to question three specific things about God. He caused her to question (1) God's Word, (2) God's provision and (3) God's goodness.

Did you notice that Satan began his conversation with Eve by asking a question? This was not an accident. He was crafty and cunning. He knew that the best way to begin a rebellion was to ask a question. It was a simple but pointed question: "Did God actually say…?" Satan began his attack on God's kingdom by questioning God's Word. We must never forget that Satan is as familiar with God's Word as the most seasoned biblical scholar. In fact, in his temptation of Jesus (Matthew 4:1-11) he even quotes Scripture!

Satan moved from questioning God's Word to insinuating that God's provision for Adam and Eve was insignificant. What an absurd thought! God had provided Adam and Eve with everything they needed to enjoy the best spinach salad ever created. But, the text tells us that Eve saw that the fruit of the tree of the knowledge of good and evil was "good for food" and "a delight to the eyes."

In her estimation, what God had provided was just simply not good enough.

Then, Satan threw in the kicker – "Eve, God is holding out on you!" He questioned God's goodness, calling him a liar and a deceiver. Satan declared that the only reason God gave them this command was to keep them from becoming like him. He reduced God to nothing more than a cosmic ogre seeking to maintain his position of authority.

Eve caved to Satan's cunning and crafty rebellion and ate the forbidden fruit. Lest all the blame be laid at her feet, the text says, "she also gave some to her husband *who was with her*, and he ate" (italics mine). Adam stood idly by while the serpent tempted his wife and then joined the rebellion against God without protest.

SATAN BRINGS DESTRUCTION

The results of this rebellion were disastrous. The relationship Adam and Eve enjoyed with God before this event was radically altered. They immediately experienced the immense shame of sin, attempted to cover themselves with fig leaves and tried to hide from an omniscient and omnipresent God. When God came to them and began asking questions, Adam and Eve turned on one another and waved flags of personal innocence. Adam blamed Eve and she blamed the serpent.

Satan's deception brought destruction. God is true to his word and, in that moment, Adam and Eve knew what it meant to die spiritually. They would later understand what it would mean to die physically as God removed them from the Garden of Eden and access to the tree of life. He also pronounced judgment on Adam, Eve, and the serpent. God promised that Adam would toil and sweat to bring sustenance from the earth and Eve would experience pain in childbirth and desire her husband's position of authority. The most important pronouncement of judgment was issued to the serpent; he would spend his entire life cursed, slithering on the ground and would be crushed by the seed of woman. Theologians call this the protoevangelium – the first gospel. God, in his judgment of the serpent, issued the promise of a coming Messiah, one who would save his people from sin.

Ever since that day in the garden Satan has done everything within his power to disrupt God's redemption plan. Knowing that marriage and family would be key to God fulfilling his mission to bring the Messiah ("the seed of woman"), Satan has worked overtime to destroy both. What began with Adam and Eve has continued for thousands of years. Marriages and families have always been and will always be under attack!

WHY FAMILIES?

God promised that he would send a redeemer to "crush the head of the serpent" but he also noted that the serpent would "bruise" his heel. Throughout the Old Testament we see Satan working to bring God's redemption plan to ruin. How did he attempt to accomplish this objective? He attacked marriages and families. There is a tremendous amount of dysfunction recorded in the Old Testament even with God's own people, the nation of Israel. We encounter things like incest, prostitution, polygamy, child sacrifice, and idol worship. Satan was working overtime! Yet, his plan of rebellion did not succeed. Jesus Christ was born of woman, lived a sinless life, died on the cross and rose from the grave.

You would think that this would discourage Satan from his grand plan of rebellion against God but you would be mistaken. You see, Satan has continued his assault on families for two reasons. First, he attacks Christian marriages and the institution of marriage in general because it is a picture of the gospel. Consider these words in Ephesians 5:22-33:

> *Wives, submit to your own husbands, as to the Lord. For the husband is the head of the wife even as Christ is the head of the church, his body, and is himself its Savior. Now as the church submits to Christ, so also wives should submit in everything to their husbands. Husbands, love your wives, as Christ loved the church and gave himself up for her, that he might sanctify her, having cleansed her by the washing of water with the word, so that he*

might present the church to himself in splendor, without spot or wrinkle or any such thing, that she might be holy and without blemish. In the same way husbands should love their wives as their own bodies. He who loves his wife loves himself. For no one ever hated his own flesh, but nourishes and cherishes it, just as Christ does the church, because we are members of his body. "Therefore a man shall leave his father and mother and hold fast to his wife, and the two shall become one flesh." This mystery is profound, and I am saying that it refers to Christ and the church. However, let each one of you love his wife as himself, and let the wife see that she respects her husband.

The clearest picture of Jesus' love for his church, outside the gospel narratives, is the institution of marriage. When a husband loves his wife unconditionally and she responds with honor and respect, the lost world around this Christian couple encounters the gospel message in real life. No wonder Satan is doing everything he can to destroy Christian marriages! If he can distort this picture of the gospel or even destroy it then he has hope that his continued rebellion against God might succeed. The last thing he wants is a walking billboard proclaiming the great love Jesus has for his church.

He also attacks families because they are the seedbeds for gospel proclamation. As was noted before, the first place the Great Commission should be pursued is within the home. If Satan cannot destroy Christian marriages he will attack Christian families so that the gospel is not passed from one generation to the next. The last thing Satan wants is for the gospel to spread and we can be certain that our families are fair game in his rebellious scheme.

How Does Satan Attack Families?

Satan begins his attack on families by attacking the very institution of marriage itself. God created the institution of marriage and even performed the first wedding ceremony between Adam and Eve in Genesis 2:18-25. Not long after God brought Adam and Eve together, Satan unleashed his deceptive and rebellious plan. The beautiful institution of marriage God established quickly became a battlefield. Sin ravaged their relationship: they ran from God, attempted to cover up their sin and shame and blamed one another for their sin.

Since that time, every marriage is comprised of two sinners saying, "I do." What began with the first married couple in the Garden of Eden has continued to this day. Satan continues to attack marriages. Through numerous schemes he convinces people that marriage is primarily about their personal happiness instead of God's glory and spouses walk away from their marriage so they can pursue "happiness." Satan knows that one of the keys to disrupting the spread of the gospel within the home is to destroy marriages. He is relentless and he is ruthless. We see this in rampant divorce (even among Christian couples), the pervasiveness of pornography and sensuality in our culture, the celebration of adultery in media and the current debate over homosexual "marriage."

We are also witnessing Satan attack Christian families. Many parents have sacrificed the ability to disciple their children on the altar of busyness. We have bought the lie that our kids are successful because they are brilliant students and phenomenal athletes. We often pour all of our effort, energy and time into securing our kid's "futures" while wholesale neglecting their spiritual growth and development. Parents are also tempted to abdicate their responsibility and expect churches to step in to teach and train their children in the ways of the Lord.

Broken and ineffective marriages mar the beautiful picture of the gospel (Jesus' love for his church) and inhibit its spread. Busy, distracted parents neglect to train their children in the ways of the Lord, leading to a generation of "Christian kids" who do not know Jesus or the Scriptures. The alarm must be sounded – we must recognize that we are under attack!

Is There Hope?

You may have reached this point in the book and wondered if there is hope. If we are in a "no holds barred" wrestling match with the evil one, is it possible for us to save our marriages, disciple our children and make an impact for God's kingdom? The good news of the gospel is that our victory over Satan is guaranteed and the Holy Spirit empowers us to follow God's plan daily. However, we must get our heads out of the sand and prepare to do battle on behalf of our marriages and families.

QUESTIONS FOR FAMILIES TO CONSIDER

In light of what we have discussed in this chapter, I want to encourage you to consider the questions below. I believe the answers to these questions will reveal a great deal about the state of your marriage/family. Ultimately, I hope answering these questions prepares you to consider how vitally important a healthy marriage and family are to raising children who know God and his Word.

1. Do you recognize that you and your family are involved in a daily spiritual battle?
2. What are some areas of weakness that you see in your marriage that could be exploited?
3. What steps do you take to help fortify your marriage/family against the attacks of Satan?
4. Does your family tend to emphasize cultural success (sports, academics, etc.) over spiritual development and growth in the lives of your children?
5. What are you currently doing to help your children develop a relationship with Jesus Christ and grow spiritually?

QUESTIONS FOR CHURCHES TO CONSIDER

My hope and prayer has been that church leaders would take the time to read this book and consider its implications for ministry. If you are a church leader, I encourage you to honestly answer the questions below with regards to your ministry setting. I believe your answers will serve as the starting point from which you can encourage families to take seriously their responsibility to be actively involved in the spiritual growth and development of their children.

1. Does your church recognize the battle that your couples/ families are in on a daily basis?
2. What is your church doing to help strengthen marriages? Do couples know about these opportunities?
3. What resources does your church offer married couples that are struggling in their marriage? Do couples know these resources are available?
4. Does your church seek to equip parents to fulfill their role of being actively involved in their child's spiritual growth and development?

2

HOUSTON... WE HAVE A HUGE PROBLEM!

I love to read history books, specifically books on the Revolutionary War and Civil War. I'm fascinated by many of our country's greatest leaders (George Washington, John Adams, Patrick Henry, Abraham Lincoln, Robert E. Lee, Stonewall Jackson etc.) who strategically responded to the situations in which they found themselves. As I have read through various accounts of their lives one thing continuously reappears; these men had a clear understanding of where they were and what needed to be done.

The groundwork has been laid up to this point to help you recognize that your marriage and family are under attack. This is a reality and one we must take very seriously. However, it is not enough to know that our families are under attack. I want us to recognize where we are in this battle for the next generation. We must have a clear picture of the reality in which we find ourselves at this very moment in history.

PERCEPTION OF THE PROBLEM

In the twenty-first century, evidence suggests that Christian parents are rarely involved in the spiritual development of their children. George Barna stated, "Nationwide, fewer than one out of every ten born-again families read the Bible together during a typical week or pray together during a typical week, excluding mealtimes."[3] In his study of teenagers, Christian Smith discovered only nineteen percent of conservative Protestant teens reported that their family talks about God, the scriptures, prayer, or other religious or spiritual matters on a daily basis.[4] Alvin Reid, in his book *Raising the Bar*, wrote, "Currently, we are not raising up a generation of soldiers ready for spiritual battle."[5] There is growing concern that Christian parents have neglected to provide their children with the biblical and spiritual foundation they need.

Teenagers are largely isolated from their families and this has resulted in a difficult transition from childhood to adulthood. Mark DeVries stated that fifty years ago "teenagers and parents had little choice but to spend hours and hours together" which meant that "young people couldn't avoid observing and listening in on the adult world, giving youth exposure that laid a natural track into adulthood."[6] The isolation of teenagers has pervaded every aspect of culture and it threatens the spiritual health of both the church and society. Research indicates that somewhere between 70%-75% of teenagers who grow up in the church will leave the church within their first year of college.[7]

---

3   George Barna, *Revolutionary Parenting* (Carol Stream, IL: Tyndale Publishers, 2007), 31.

4   Christian Smith and Melinda Lundquist Denton, *Soul Searching: The Religious and Spiritual Lives of American Teenagers* (New York: Oxford University Press, 2005), 54-55.

5   Alvin Reid, *Raising the Bar: Ministry to Youth in the New Millennium* (Grand Rapids: Kregel, 2004), 44.

6   Mark DeVries, *Family-Based Youth Ministry*, 2d ed. (Downers Grove, IL: InterVarsity Press, 2004), 41.

7   https://www.barna.org/barna-update/article/16-teensnext-gen/147-most-twentysomethings-put-christianity-on-the-shelf-following-spiritually-active-teen-years#.VEkNyBbb9BU

THE PROBLEM AND YOU

It is one thing to think that the "problem" exists out there but I am confident that most Christian parents struggle to be actively involved in the spiritual lives of their children. Several years ago, when I served as a student pastor, I sensed that our parents were not discipling their children. As I sought to equip them and challenge them to take their biblical role seriously, I developed a questionnaire to help them think through this responsibility. I want to encourage you to take a few minutes and answer the questionnaire that follows as honestly as possible.

Instructions: Please fill in the blank with the number of the answer that most closely corresponds to your own practice, using a scale of 1 to 5, with 1 = Not Involved and 5 = Very Involved

1. How involved would you say you are in your child's spiritual development? _____

2. How often do you read the Bible together with your family on a weekly basis? _____

3. How often do you pray together with your family on a weekly basis, excluding mealtimes? _____

4. How often does your child come to talk to you about spiritual matters on a weekly basis? _____

5. How often do you sit down together at the table to eat (breakfast, lunch, or dinner) on a weekly basis? _____

6. How often do you discuss cultural issues with your child (i.e. news, movies, books, etc.)? _____

7.   How often do you pray for your child on a weekly basis?

_____

Circle the letter answer that most closely corresponds to your own practice.

1)   In the course of a typical week, how often do you spend in Bible study and prayer?
   a)   daily
   b)   a couple of times a week
   c)   once a week
   d)   never

2)   In the course of a typical week, how much television do you watch?
   a)   1-5 hours
   b)   5-10 hours
   c)   10-15 hours
   d)   15-20 hours
   e)   more than 20 hours
   f)   I do not watch television

3)   In the course of a typical week, how much time do you spend with your child/children?
   a)   1-5 hours
   b)   5-10 hours
   c)   10-15 hours
   d)   15-20 hours
   e)   more than 20 hours

Answer the following questions by circling True or False.

1)   True / False   Absolute moral truth exists.

2)   True / False   Jesus Christ lived a sinless life during his earthly ministry.

3)   True / False   God created the universe and continues to rule it today.

4)   True / False   Salvation can be earned by good works.

5)   True / False   The Bible contains some errors.

6)   True / False   The Bible teaches the doctrine of the Trinity.

7)   True / False   Jesus Christ was born of a virgin.

8)   True / False   Miracles recorded in the Bible are not true.

9)   True / False   Christians should share the gospel with non-believers.

10)   True / False   Satan is not a real living entity.

Please write your answers in the space provided.

1)   What are your goals for your child/children? _____

_____
_____
_____
_____
_____
_____

2)   Do you have a plan for being involved in your child's/children's spiritual development? Please explain your answer. _____

_____
_____
_____
_____
_____
_____

3) Do you believe your child/children has/have a biblical worldview? Please explain your answer. _____

_____

_____

_____

_____

_____

_____

4) What are some biblical references that specifically discuss the relationship between parents and children? _____

_____

_____

_____

_____

_____

_____

5) What do you think should be the type of relationship between Christian parents and the church? _____

_____

_____

_____

_____

_____

How did you do? This questionnaire is set up to examine several aspects of the relationship between parents, children and churches. The first ten questions expose our basic relationship with our children when it comes to spiritual matters. Do we spend time together with our children discussing spiritual matters? Do we read the Bible together? Do we pray for our children? The next ten questions examine where we are spiritually. If we have the responsibility to disciple our children, the question we must ask is whether or not we are disciples of Jesus? Do we have a biblical worldview that has permeated our lives and that we can pass along to our children? The final five questions are a bit more involved and require us to look at the specific plan we have to be actively involved in the spiritual lives of our children. Many of us have great plans for our children academically, vocationally, and culturally but do we have great plans for them spiritually?

WHERE DO WE GO FROM HERE?

It is essential for parents to recognize their biblical responsibility to drive the discipleship process while also partnering together with the local church as they disciple their children. Most Christian parents do not have a firm grasp on the biblical texts that address the relationship between parents and children/teenagers. It is essential to establish this foundation because Scripture indicates that parents have the primary responsibility to teach and train their children in the ways of the Lord.

Paul Tripp encouraged parents to know and accept that "God intended the family to be his primary learning community, parents to be his primary teachers, and family life to be just the right context for life instruction to take place."[8] He insisted that this will take work and that parents must devote themselves to understanding both the biblical responsibility they have and the teenagers they are seeking to train.[9] If parents fail to recognize this responsibility, the primary training for children will not be accomplished in the home.

Dennis and Barbara Rainey noted that "parents fulfill many important roles for their children: cook, innkeeper, medic, taxi driver, coach," however, "there's one role that is often overlooked or misunderstood – disciple maker."[10] The task of making disciples was given by Jesus in Matthew 28:19-20 and parents should see

---

8 Paul David Tripp, *Age of Opportunity: A Biblical Guide to Parenting Teens* (Phillipsburg, NJ: P & R Publishing, 2001), 42.

9 Ibid., 43-51.

10 Dennis and Barbara Rainey, *Growing a Spiritually Strong Family* (Colorado Springs: Multnomah, 2002), 61.

the family as the primary place to begin this mission.[11] Voddie Baucham insisted that it is time for parents to assume this responsibility and accomplish the task God has set before them.[12]

THE ROAD AHEAD

I fully recognize that what we have covered may be overwhelming if this is the first time you have been confronted with your biblical calling as a parent or the first time you have seriously thought about this responsibility. The questionnaire above may have exposed weaknesses and concerns in your family life. It would be easy at this point to shut the book and walk away but I want to encourage you to press on and look at how the Scriptures define your responsibility as a parent.

---

11 Ibid.
12 Voddie Baucham, *Family Driven Faith*, (Wheaton, IL: Crossway, 2007), 92.

3

TRAIN UP A CHILD: BLESSING AND RESPONSIBILITY

In the last chapter, we looked at where we are currently in our culture and I want to focus this chapter on the biblical responsibility parents have to be involved in their children's spiritual growth and development. We are going to dive into Scripture throughout the next several pages so I would encourage you to grab your Bible, a notebook and a pen to prepare for this journey. Also, take some time before you continue reading and ask that God would open your eyes to His truth (Psalm 119:18). There should be great joy, as we study these passages, to know, "All Scripture is breathed out by God and profitable for teaching, for reproof, for correction, and for training in righteousness, that the man of God may be complete, equipped for every good work."[13]

THE BIBLICAL RATIONALE FOR PARENT-DRIVEN DISCIPLESHIP

Scripture emphasizes the need for parents to be involved in the spiritual development of their children. Ligon Duncan stated, "The family is God's divinely appointed 'small group' discipleship

---

13 2 Timothy 3:16-17

program."[14] In Genesis 1:26-28, God instituted the family and gave
Adam and Eve the charge, "Be fruitful and multiply and fill the
earth and subdue it and have dominion over the fish of the sea and
over the birds of the heavens and over every living thing that moves
on the earth."[15] The command to be fruitful and multiply was given
by God in order to demonstrate his blessing upon the family. In
Jewish culture, children were seen as a blessing directly from God.
Kenneth Matthews wrote, "This notion of blessing associated with
reproduction is a constant in Israel, where children are seen as the
providential favor of the Lord."[16] The Psalmist wrote, in Psalm
127:3-5, that "children are a heritage from the Lord" and "the fruit
of the womb a reward." This passage further emphasizes the fact
that children are a gift from God and it states that parents with
children should consider themselves blessed. This blessing, however, also brought with it a great responsibility. Parents were expected
to raise their children in the ways of the Lord and the family was
at the centerpiece of God's discipleship program. Duncan stated,
"God has never underestimated the importance of the family" and
"it is the normal school in which faith in God and obedience to
his law are taught."[17] Scripture indicates that the family should
serve as the place where biblical truth is taught. This responsibility
is assigned in the Old Testament and emphasized in the New Testament. Andreas Kostenberger wrote, "The Pentateuch, the Old
Testament historical books, and the book of Psalms are pervaded
by the consciousness that parents (and especially fathers) must pass
on their religious heritage to their children."[18] This instruction was

---

14 Ligon Duncan, "A Call to Family Worship," *Journal of Biblical Manhood
   and Womanhood* 9:1 (Spring 2004): 8.
15 Genesis 1:28.
16 Kenneth Matthews, *Genesis 1-11:26.* in *The New American Commentary*,
   ed. E. Ray Clendenen, vol. 1 (Nashville: Broadman and Holman, 1996),
   174.
17 Duncan, "A Call to Family Worship," 7.
18 Andreas Kostenberger and David Jones, *God Marriage and Family:
   Rebuilding the Biblical Foundation* (Wheaton: Crossway Books, 2004),
   103.

the primary means whereby parents could instill faith in God and obedience to His prescribed standards.

Scripture indicates that this also should be the desire of every Christian parent. John MacArthur emphasized this when he wrote, "What we desperately need is a return to biblical principles of parenting."[19] He further stated that the principles found in Scripture need to be applied and obeyed.[20] Both the Old Testament and New Testament contain specific passages that stress the importance of parental discipleship and we will spend the next several pages looking at these pertinent passages.

OLD TESTAMENT PASSAGES

Exodus 12:1-51

Chapter 12 in Exodus offers evidence of the responsibility parents have to teach their children concerning the work of God in history. Moses was given the command by God to instruct the people to prepare their homes so that the angel of the Lord would pass over and not destroy the first-born child. One of the most important aspects of this command was its direct implication on the life of the nation of Israel. F. C. Cook stated, "The Passover was to be a memorial, a commerative and sacramental ordinance of perpetual obligation."[21] This command inaugurated the Feast of the Passover whereby the nation of Israel reflected upon God's deliverance and provision. C. F. Keil further emphasized the importance of the Passover when he wrote, "The commemoration of that act was to be an eternal ordinance, and to be upheld as long as Israel should exist as the redeemed people of the Lord."[22] The

---

19 John MacArthur, *What the Bible Says About Parenting* (Nashville: Word Publishing, 2000), xi.

20 Ibid.

21 F. C. Cook, ed., *Genesis to Deuteronomy*, in *The Bible Commentary*, vol. 1 (Grand Rapids: Baker Book House, 1981), 295.

22 C. F. Keil, *The Pentateuch*, in *Commentary on the Old Testament*, vol. 1, C. F. Keil and F. Delitzsch eds. (Peabody: Hendrickson Publishers, 2006), 332.

Passover gave the nation of Israel the opportunity and privilege to celebrate what God had done on their behalf.

A key aspect of Moses' command focused on the responsibility of parents to teach their children the reason for participating in the Passover celebration. This is evident in Exodus 12:14 when Moses wrote, "This day shall be for you a memorial day, and you shall keep it as a feast to the Lord; throughout your generations, as a statue forever, you shall keep it as a feast." The purpose of instituting the Passover was to offer a specific opportunity for parents to instruct their children concerning God's deliverance. Warren Wiersbe wrote that the Passover was "a 'memorial' to be celebrated to keep alive in Israel the story of the Exodus (v. 14; 13:8-10)."[23] According to Wiersbe, this would allow "Jewish parents another opportunity to teach their children the meaning of their freedom and what God did for them."[24] The annual celebration was instituted because it provided a means whereby parents could teach their children how God had worked in their nation's history. God's desire to establish the Passover displays the necessity for parents to take the time to instruct their children concerning God's actions in history.

Deuteronomy 6:1-9, 20-25

Any discussion concerning the responsibility of parents to disciple their children largely will be grounded on Deuteronomy 6:1-9 and 20-25. In it, Moses gave the foundation of the Jewish faith and told how this faith should be transmitted to future generations. Bruce Willoughby wrote, "Verses 4-9 were the primary confession of faith supplemented by Deuteronomy 11:13-21 and Numbers 15:37-41."[25] The Shema was the Jewish confession of faith and it was given to Israel after Moses had reminded them of the Ten Commandments. This was a command from God that

---

23 Warren Wiersbe, ed., *Old Testament: Genesis – Deuteronomy*, in *The Bible Exposition Commentary*, vol. 1 (Colorado Springs: Victor, 2001), 199.

24 Ibid.

25 Bruce E. Willoughby, "A Heartfelt Love: An Exegesis of Deuteronomy 6:4-19," *Restoration Quarterly* 20, no. 2 (1997): 77.

urged Israel to stand firm on the truth He had already given them and challenged them to instruct their children in His ways.

The command to instruct children is foundational in this passage and emphasizes the need for parental discipleship. Roy Zuck stated that the Lord commands parents to be "intense, diligent, earnest, and consistent" in teaching their children and they "dare not be haphazard, negligent, or halfhearted in the training of their children."[26] Robert Jamieson, A. R. Fausset, and David Brown discussed the role of parents outlined in this passage when they wrote, "They were enjoined to instruct their children from infancy (Isa. xxviii. 9) in the Decalogue and other principal parts of the law by speaking on every suitable occasion."[27] The responsibility of parents was to be intentional in teaching their children the ways of the Lord. This was not a suggestion that they should follow but a command directly given to parents by God.

Moses further emphasized this charge to parents in Deuteronomy 6:20-25. Keil wrote, "In vv. 20-25, the teaching to the children, which is only briefly hinted at in v. 7, is more fully explained."[28] This further explanation encouraged parents to teach about God's provision in order "to awaken in the younger generation love to the Lord and to His commandments."[29] The expectation in this passage is that parents will teach their children for the purpose of ensuring that future generations will remember the commands and works of the Lord. Daniel Block emphasized that while this passage is not long, it is significant because it offers guidance in the way Christian parents transmit the faith to their children. He stated that this text "highlights the importance of deliberate strategies for transmitting the faith" and "teaches clearly the relationship between law and grace within the divine plan of salvation and sanctifica-

---

26 Roy B. Zuck, "Hebrew Words for 'Teach'," *Bibliotheca Sacra* 121:483 (July 1964): 235

27 Robert Jamieson, A. R. Fausset, and David Brown, eds., *Genesis – Esther*, in *Jamieson-Fausset-Brown Bible Commentary*, vol. 1 (Peabody: Hendrickson Publishers, 2002), 637.

28 Keil, *The Pentateuch*, 886.

29 Ibid.

tion."[30] Verses 20-25 emphasize the responsibility parents have to train their children and how essential and necessary this is in the faith community.

This text is of fundamental importance to the Christian family even though, in its immediate context, it is directly given to the nation of Israel. Andreas Kostenberger believes that parents have the primary responsibility to teach children their religious heritage and stated, "God's express will for his people Israel is still his will for God's people in the church today."[31] This passage of Scripture contains a command for parents to disciple their children and instruct them concerning the Christian faith. Parents in the church, like the parents in Israel, should heed this command and seek to train their children in the ways of the Lord.

Joshua 4:4-7

The reaction to one of the most important events in Israel's history is examined in this text. In the previous chapter Joshua had prepared and led the people of Israel to cross the Jordan River and enter the Promised Land. Donald Campbell noted that this event was of monumental importance in Jewish history because it was the point when God's people were finally able to fulfill the promise God had given to Moses before the exodus.[32] The final test of their faith was dependent upon God to provide a way for them to cross the Jordan River. God accomplished this supernaturally by stopping the flow of the river, which allowed the people to cross on dry ground.[33]

In chapter four, Joshua gave the command to build a memorial in order for the people to remember this event and teach future generations about God's deliverance. Warren Wiersbe noted that

30 Daniel I. Block, "The Grace of Torah: The Mosaic Prescription for Life (Deut. 4:1-8; 6:20-25)," *Bibliotheca Sacra* 162:645 (Jan. 2005): 4.

31 Kostenberger and Jones, *God, Marriage, and Family*, 102.

32 Donald K. Campbell, *Joshua*, in *The Bible Knowledge Commentary*, vol. 1, John F. Walvoord and Roy B. Zuck eds. (Colorado Springs: Victor, 2000), 334.

33 Ibid., 335.

twelve stones were gathered by twelve chosen men and placed in Gilgal so that the people of Israel could teach "the next generation about Jehovah and His special relationship to the people of Israel."[34] Donald Madvig stated this memorial of stones was set up specifically for future generations to be "told the story as if the event had happened to them personally so that they could participate in all that God had done for Israel."[35]

This memorial served as a means whereby parents could teach their children concerning God's deliverance and provision. Matthew Henry believed that this same practice is useful for Christian parents today. He wrote, "God's mercies to our ancestors were mercies to us; and we should take all occasions to revive the remembrance of the great things God did for our fathers in the days of old."[36] Joshua established this memorial so that future generations could be taught about God's provision and parents today should likewise teach children concerning God's work in the past. This will offer an opportunity for children to understand the work of God in history and how this work has specifically affected them.

Psalm 78:1-11

Psalm 78, written by Asaph, contains an encouragement to teach future generations the works of God so that they would not forget what he had done. Kostenberger stated, "Thus, from generation to generation, God's ways and will are to be passed on for children to learn from the sins of their fathers and for God to be known as mighty and glorious."[37] Particular attention is given to the need of reminding future generations of the sins and failures of previous generations. John Phillips wrote, "Of all the attitudes a parent can adopt, the worst surely is to say, as so many do: 'I am

---

34 Warren Wiersbe, ed., *Old Testament History*, in *The Bible Exposition Commentary*, vol. 2 (Colorado Springs: Victor, 2003), 33.

35 Donald H. Madvig, *Joshua*, in *The Expositor's Bible Commentary*, vol. 3, Frank E. Gaebelien ed. (Grand Rapids: Zondervan, 1992), 272.

36 Matthew Henry, ed., *Joshua to Esther*, in *Matthew Henry's Commentary*, vol. 2 (McLean: MacDonald Publishing Company, nd), 22.

37 Kostenberger and Jones, *God, Marriage, and Family*, 102.

not going to force religion on my children. I am going to let them make up their own minds when they are old enough.'"[38] He further emphasized that if parents teach their children the ways of the Lord then generation after generation will fear the Lord and He will bless them. If parents fail to teach their children the ways of the Lord, however, then the character of society will disintegrate.[39]

James Montgomery Boice emphasized that this charge to parents is not new. Asaph is simply reiterating the command given to the generation of the exodus.[40] The need for parents to train their children and teach them about the works of God remained essential in the life of the nation of Israel. Boice stated, "We have a duty to do this because God has commanded us to do it (v. 5), and we should also want to do it because it is the means by which our children may come to 'put their trust in God' and 'not forget his deeds' (v. 7)."[41] The faithfulness of the Israelites was related directly to their obedience to God's command. If they taught generation after generation the works of the Lord then they had good reason to believe that these future generations would continue in obedience to God. Charles Spurgeon noted that when this happens "a golden chain be formed, wherewith being bound together, the whole family may seek the skies."[42] The psalmist's words reminded parents to train and teach their children all that God had done and the dire consequences of rejecting his ways.

Proverbs 22:6

Proverbs 22:6 is of fundamental importance when evaluating the responsibility parents have to train and disciple their children. Ted Hildebrandt stated, "This proverb is cited in support of a pleth-

---

38 John Phillips, *Exploring Psalms: Volume One*, in *The John Phillips Commentary Series* (Grand Rapids: Kregel, 1988), 644-645.

39 Phillips, *Exploring Psalms*, 644-645.

40 James Montgomery Boice, *Psalms 42-106: An Expositional Commentary* (Grand Rapids: Baker, 1996), 645.

41 Ibid.

42 Charles Spurgeon, *The Treasury of David: Classic Reflections on the Wisdom of the Psalms*, vol. 2 (Peabody: Hendrickson, nd), 350.

ora of educational and developmental child-rearing philosophies, paradigms and programs."[43] R. L. Roberts believed that this proverb is quoted more frequently than all proverbs and is also the one that is repeatedly misapplied.[44] Even though there has been confusion concerning this passage, it is necessary to evaluate it when discussing the responsibility parents have in the spiritual development of their children.

The first part of this verse instructs parents to train their children. Cook stated the word train primarily means "to press into, initiate, and so, to educate."[45] Phillips wrote, "The word suggests a picture of cattle being guided into a pen." Parents have the responsibility to teach and guide their children in the ways of the Lord. This teaching and guiding should be intentional and be started early in the child's life. Gordon Lovik stated, "This verse maintains that the parent is to educate the child at every stage of life, but especially in the early years."[46] The method by which parents train their children is not fixed. In fact, F. Delitzsch believed that parents should adapt their training depending on the age of the child and his or her spiritual development.[47] These variables continue to be in flux and the responsibility of the parent is to work to understand the best way to be involved in the spiritual development of their children in each stage of life.

The desired outcome of this training is that children will continue walking in the ways of the Lord throughout their lives. One of the greatest difficulties with this passage is that some understand this verse as a promise instead of a proverb. Roberts stated, "The

43 Ted Hildebrandt, "Proverbs 22:6a - Train Up a Child?," *Grace Theological Journal* 9:1 (Spring 1988): 6.

44 R. L. Roberts, Jr., "Train Up a Child," *Restoration Quarterly* 6, no. 1 (1962): 40.

45 F. C. Cook, ed., *Job to Song of Solomon*, in *The Bible Commentary*, vol. 4 (Grand Rapids: Baker, 1981), 588.

46 John Phillips, *Exploring Proverbs: Volume Two*, in *The John Phillips Commentary Series* (Neptune: Loizeaux Brothers, 1996), 168.

47 F. Delitzsch, *Proverbs, Ecclesiastes, Song of Songs*, in *Commentary on the Old Testament*, vol. 6, C. F. Keil and F. Delitzsch eds. (Peabody: Hendrickson, 2006), 324.

usual application of the verse is that, if a child is taught the Bible and given the proper religious training, he will be faithful during the remaining years of his life.[48] The problem with applying this in such a manner is that experience seems to indicate that there is no guarantee children will continue walking in the ways of the Lord even when parents properly train them. This proverb, however, encourages parents that they still have the responsibility to train their children even if the desired result is not obtained.

New Testament Passages

Ephesians 6:1-4

Paul addressed the relationship between parents and children in Ephesians 6:1-4. He first wrote concerning the responsibility children have to obey their parents. This was the fifth command given by Moses to the Israelites and Paul saw the necessity to pass it along to his Gentile audience. The second aspect of this passage focused on the responsibility parents have to train their children in righteousness without provoking them to anger. John MacArthur believes this aspect of Paul's letter would have been new teaching to the Ephesians. He stated that fathers had complete control over their children and children were viewed no differently than slaves.[49] A. Skevington Wood wrote, "In a society where the father's authority (patria potestas) was absolute, this represented a revolutionary concept.[50] Paul addressed the fact that parents have the responsibility to train and educate their children without provoking them to anger.

The duty of the parent is stated negatively and positively. They are not to provoke their children to anger but bring them up in the training and admonition of the Lord. Oliver Greene wrote that the positive aspect of training children should be accomplished through

---

48 R. L. Roberts, Jr. "Train Up a Child," 40.

49 John MacArthur, ed., *Ephesians*, in *The MacArthur New Testament Commentary* (Chicago: Moody Press, 1986), 314-315.

50 A. Skevington Wood, *Ephesians*, in *The Expositor's Bible Commentary*, vol. 11, Frank E. Gaebelien ed. (Grand Rapids: Zondervan, 1981), 81.

Bible reading, family prayer, and active participation in church. He went on to note that great churches are built with great families.[51] The responsibility of parents is to make sure they are providing for both the child's physical and spiritual needs. Moses gave this command to the Israelites and Paul reminds Christian parents that this applies to them as well.

Colossians 3:21

Colossians 3:21 is similar to Ephesians 6:4 but only contains the negative command that parents should not provoke their children to wrath. Kostenberger wrote that parents are "not to use their position of authority to exasperate their children, but to treat them with gentleness."[52] Wiersbe believes Christian children need to be encouraged in light of the difficult world they are living in and that the home should be the happiest environment for them. He stated, "Christian parents must listen carefully, share the feelings and frustrations of their children, pray with them, and seek to encourage them."[53] This takes intentionality but it is the task God has given to parents. They should have a relationship with their child that employs teaching and discipline while also maintaining an environment of encouragement.

One mistake parents can make is belittling their children when they discipline. Parents do have the responsibility to discipline their children but it should be done in such a way that it does not provoke them to anger. Melick wrote, "Parents embitter children by constantly picking at them, perhaps refusing to acknowledge their efforts."[54] Paul reminded parents that the goal is to train their child in the ways of the Lord and encourage them throughout the

---

51 Oliver B. Greene, *The Epistle of Paul the Apostle to the Ephesians* (Greenville: The Gospel Hour, 1963), 197-198.

52 Kostenberger and Jones, *God, Marriage, and Family*, 119.

53 Warren Wiersbe, *New Testament: Volume Two*, in *The Bible Exposition Commentary*, vol. 6 (Colorado Springs: Victor, 2001), 143.

54 Richard R. Melick, Jr., *Philippians, Colossians, Philemon*, in *The New American Commentary*, vol. 32, David S. Dockery ed. (Nashville: Broadman Press, 1991), 315.

process. Curtis Vaughan believes that parents can be "so exacting, so demanding, or so severe that they create within their children the feeling that it is impossible for them to please."[55] Paul encouraged parents to exercise their authority without allowing this to happen. Instead, they should parent in such a way that encourages the child whether the child is being instructed or disciplined.

AN EASY YOKE & LIGHT BURDEN

I know we covered a ton of ground over the last few pages but my intent was to help you see the comprehensive way in which Scripture challenges parents to take a primary role in discipling their children. At this point, some of you may feel overwhelmed with the burden of this responsibility but I want to offer you some encouragement. Jesus said, in Matthew 11:28-30, "Come to me, all who labor and are heavy laden, and I will give you rest. Take my yoke upon you, and learn from me, for I am gentle and lowly in heart, and you will find rest for your souls. For my yoke is easy, and my burden is light." God is gracious to us even in our feeble attempts to fulfill this responsibility and the great news is that he is at work in and through us during the entire process!

---

55 Curtis Vaughan, *Colossians*, in *The Expositor's Bible Commentary*, vol. 11, Frank E. Gaebelein ed. (Grand Rapids: Zondervan, 1981), 219.

CULTIVATING A GOSPEL-CENTERED HOME

I don't know about you but I am a nuts and bolts kind of person. Ideas are wonderful but I'm more concerned with actually seeing ideas come to life. The idea of making disciples at home sounds great and it is biblical. But, I'm sure you are asking a very simple question, "How do I do it?" "What steps can I take to help me accomplish the vital calling given to me by God?"

I think the simplest answer to those questions is to seek to cultivate a gospel-centered home. By this I mean that parents should take every opportunity to magnify Jesus Christ and his saving gospel in their home and with their children. In our home we have chosen to think about this in two basic categories: (1) Rhythms and (2) Rites of Passage.

RHYTHMS

I recently read a blog post by Doug Wilson that emphasized the concept of plodding as it related to productivity. He wrote, "I believe in plodding. Productivity is more a matter of diligent, long-distance hiking that it is one hundred-yard dashing. Doing a little bit now is far better than hoping to do a lot on the morrow. So redeem the fifteen minute spaces."[56] The same holds true for cultivating a gospel-centered home and teaching our children about the Lord. We need to redeem the moments in the rhythms of life. In Deuteronomy 6, Moses encouraged the Israelites to discuss spiritual matters with their children diligently during every day life *("when you sit in your house, and when you walk by the way, and when you lie down, and when you rise")* and we should identify those regular rhythms in our lives and leverage them for maximum impact. Here are a few rhythms that we have identified in our own family that we have sought to use to cultivate a gospel-centered home.

Family Dinner

We do everything in our power to eat together as a family every night. By this I mean we all sit down at the kitchen table and spend time together talking over our meal without the interruption of television or any other electronic device. This offers us a wonderful opportunity to talk to our children about their day, what they are learning, and discuss any other tidbits they want to share.

I am constantly amazed at how our conversations over dinner open the door to discuss spiritual matters. It may be something as simple as talking about how God made the moon and stars or how treating our friends kindly is good and right. These are not rigid or forced conversation where we hijack the moment and try to toss Jesus in the midst. We do, however, try to take every opportunity to point our girls to Christ in every conversation and every situation.

Do you eat dinner together as a family? If you do, have you taken this prime opportunity to discuss spiritual matters with your children? I want to challenge you to make dinner with your family a priority each night and look for opportunities to point your kids to Christ as they open up about their day.

---

56 http://dougwils.com/s7-engaging-the-culture/the-fruitfulness-of-plodding.html

FAMILY WORSHIP

We did not have family worship in my home growing up. I don't believe my parents had any idea what it was and, to be perfectly honest, neither did I until I read a little book in seminary by Don Whitney, *Family Worship: In the Bible, In History and In Your Home*. If you have no experience with family worship I would encourage you to pick up his book and take some time to work through it with your family.

Family worship is simply a time set aside where families gather together to sing, read Scripture and pray. Throughout the history of the church, worshiping together as a family was a common practice that was greatly encouraged. Many pastors wrote devotionals and catechisms for parents to use at home and Puritan pastors were even known to take the time to visit church members in their homes and train fathers to lead family worship.

Our practice of family worship has changed as our kids have gotten older but the basic format has remained the same. We usually begin our time together singing some type of worship song. Often we let our kids pick the song and they love to sing songs that they have learned at church. Next, we take time to read the Scriptures and talk about what we have read (We have enjoyed using the *Jesus Storybook Bible* since it is geared towards children). We close out our time together spending time in prayer for our family/friends, our church and our world.

Let me quickly dispel any notion that this time is calm and peaceful. With younger kids family worship is often chaotic. There are moments when they are not paying attention and when we have to discipline them but this is one of their favorite times of the day. My wife and I love to hear them sing and pray. We are encouraged as they ask and answer questions. Ultimately, I know that this daily time together is laying the foundation for their future walk with Christ.

Do you currently have family worship? It does not have to be an extravagant affair and if you have small kids it will likely not last very long. But, I am confident that the seeds planted in our children's lives through these moments will bear fruit in years to come.

WEEKLY WORSHIP

Another way to cultivate a gospel-centered home is to make sure your family is actively involved in a local church. The author of Hebrews wrote, "Let us hold fast the confession of our hope without wavering, for He who promised is faithful. And let us consider how to stir up one another to love and good works, not neglecting to meet together, as is the habit of some, but encouraging one another, and all the more as you see the Day drawing near."[57] Too often church involvement is not a priority in the life of the family and children quickly recognize this reality. We may tell our children that church is important but we must model it for them as well.

I was saved at the age of eight and sensed a call to vocational ministry at the age of fourteen. I grew up in a great church, one where I knew the people and they truly knew me. I was baptized at this church, preached my first sermon in this church and was even married in this church. Those were some of the greatest years of my life and the people there mean the absolute world to me. They prayed with me and cried with me, encouraged me and pushed me. A large part of who I am today is a direct result of the church I grew up in. I struggled with God's call on my life and I have no doubt that the prayers of my parents and the people in this church availed much. He drew me back to Himself and the people at this church celebrated with me.

Your child needs the encouragement and love of fellow believers. This can come from other children their own age as well as adults. That is the beauty of the body of believers:

> *And he gave the apostles, the prophets, the evangelists, the*
> *shepherds and teachers, to equip the saints for the work of ministry,*
> *for building up the body of Christ, until we all attain to the unity*
> *of the faith and of the knowledge of the Son of God, to mature*
> *manhood, to the measure of the stature of the fullness of Christ, so*

---

57 Hebrews 10:23-25

that we may no longer be children, tossed to and fro by the waves and carried about by every wind of doctrine, by human cunning, by craftiness in deceitful schemes. Rather, speaking the truth in love, we are to grow up in every way into him who is the head, into Christ, from whom the whole body, joined and held together by every joint with which it is equipped, when each part is working properly, makes the body grow so that it builds itself up in love.[58]

Help fan the gospel flame in the lives of your children by making sure your family is actively involved in a local church. If your desire is that you children love Jesus then let them see you love him and his bride. They will do what they see you do and if you tell them that church is important but your actions say otherwise, they will not believe church involvement is very important. I'm not advocating legalism in church attendance but I do believe we have a responsibility to make sure our family is actively involved in a local church.

REDEEMING MOMENTS

Lastly, in the rhythm of daily life, my wife and I look for ordinary moments to point our kids to Jesus. I like to refer to these as redeeming moments. There are hundreds of opportunities like this that pass in front of us every week and we try to leverage them for the cause of the gospel.

I have the privilege of taking my oldest daughter to school every day and during our ten-minute ride we get to talk. The conversations are varied and oftentimes silly but one morning Anna asked a question most kids ask. She said, "Daddy, why is the sky blue?" I took a chemistry class in college and my mind immediately went to one of the lectures where we talked about this very thing. Since I didn't have enough time to unpack that lecture for her, I simply said, "That's just the way God made it." I almost left it at that but then I began to talk about how God created the sky and the sun and the moon all. We talked about how all of creation declares the glory of God every second of every day (Psalm 19). That led to

---

58 Ephesians 4:11-16

us talking about God creating mankind, which ultimately led to us talking about the gospel.

Most of us have heard the old adage "carpe diem" or "seize the day." As parents, we need to "seize the moments." I want to challenge you to leverage everyday moments with your children and take the opportunity to point them to Christ in these moments.

RITES OF PASSAGE

You may have never heard of a rite of passage but it is simply taking the opportunity to celebrate an important stage or defining moment in a person's life. My wife and I have identified four important stages in our daughter's lives that we plan to celebrate as they relate to their spiritual growth. We want to make certain that these are special moments in their lives that they are able to look back on years later and cherish. More importantly, my wife and I want to use these milestones to teach our girls about who God is and what He is doing in their life. Here are some of important stages and defining moments we want to celebrate:

SALVATION

I can think of no better time to celebrate than when one of your children comes to know Jesus Christ as his or her Lord and Savior. The Bible tells us that all of heaven rejoices when one sinner repents (Luke 15:10) and, if heaven is rejoicing, I believe we should rejoice as well. We should celebrate when our children move from spiritual death to spiritual life and they need to know how special this day is every year.

There are a number of ways to celebrate this occasion and I would encourage you to be creative with your children as you celebrate. As a pastor, I know many young adults who struggle with assurance of salvation and I think celebrating this yearly would allow them to go back in time to the moment they placed their faith in Jesus for their salvation. My girls have not trusted in Jesus Christ for their salvation yet but I am praying and looking forward to celebrating with them soon. What is your plan for marking this momentous occasion in your child's life?

TEENAGE YEARS

One of the most difficult times for children and parents is the dreaded teenage years. Mark Twain is said to have offered this advice concerning teenagers, "When a child turns 12, he should be kept in a barrel and fed through a hole, until he reaches 16... at which time you should plug the hole." Our girls are still young but my wife and I have made a decision that we want to make this transition memorable.

Our plan is two-fold. First, my wife and daughter will take an overnight trip together to a large city and have a girls retreat. The purpose of this retreat will be for my wife to share what it means to be a godly woman. Second, when they return, I plan to take my daughter on a daddy/daughter date and share with her what it means to be treated like a godly woman. Our hope is that these times will encourage our daughters to continue walking with the Lord as they navigate these trying years. We also want them to know that we are taking this journey with them.

MISSION TRIPS

I remember taking my first mission trip as a sixteen year old and it was one of the most impactful moments in my life. I have no doubt that this trip to Honduras cultivated a passion within me to spread the gospel and was used by God to prepare me for a life of ministry. Our hope is that our daughters will be able to have this same opportunity.

We have already begun talking with our girls about life outside of the United States and how God is at work throughout the world. We have used a prayer guide called *Operation World* during our family worship time and our oldest daughter constantly asks us when we are going to get on a plane so that we can share the gospel around the world. I can think of no better way to make disciples than to raise children who love Jesus and people all over the world that do not know him. Will you commit to the Lord that you will take your kids on a mission trip before they leave for college or the workforce?

Marriage

The final rite of passage that we have planned will happen on the night before the day our daughters get married. My wife and I have been praying for their future spouse daily and we want to celebrate this occasion with something special. I have been keeping a journal for each of our girls since they were little with thoughts, prayers and stories that I want to give them during the rehearsal dinner.

My wife and I realize that God has entrusted us with our girls for a short period of time and then he calls for us to send them out. Our prayer is that this final rite of passage will help them recognize that they are part of a legacy. They will be able to look back through their entire lives and see that mom and dad were seeking to fulfill our biblical role and responsibility in their lives. Our hope is that this is just the beginning of a legacy of the Christian faith being passed from one generation to the next.

Cultivating A Gospel Centered Home With Prayer

It would not be helpful to talk about cultivating a gospel centered home without discussing the vital importance of prayer. I want to challenge you to begin praying now for your children on a daily basis. James wrote, "The prayer of a righteous person has great power as it is working."[59] Can you imagine what the effective, fervent prayer of righteous parents will avail? I certainly can because of the prayers my parents uttered on my behalf. Shortly before Janie and I were married, my mom gave her a cookbook. Now this might not sound like much other than a mother's desire that her son will not starve but there was something special about this cookbook – a little note was written inside. It reads,

---

59 James 5:16

Dear Janie,

Wow – the big day is almost here! The Kennedy's are so excited about their soon to be daughter. I wanted to write you a little note to explain the significance of this cookbook. As you can see it was printed in 1997. At that time Michael was only 14 years old! However, I bought this book as a covenant between God and myself. When I purchased this book I started praying for Michael's future wife. My nightly prayer has always been for God to send Michael a godly, pure woman who first loves God and then loves my son with all her heart. When I met you, I knew without a doubt that you were the one! I'm so excited for you and Michael – may your lives together be everything you hope and dream for!

Wow! What an encouragement it was to have my parents praying for my future spouse and me long before our wedding day. I most definitely want to be a parent that prays for my children. How about you? Let's take a look at what Jesus said to his disciples about prayer. "Pray then like this: Our Father in heaven, hallowed be your name. Your kingdom come, your will be done, on earth as it is in heaven. Give us this day our daily bread, and forgive us our debts, as we also have forgiven our debtors. And lead us not into temptation, but deliver us from the evil."[60] Jesus tells his disciples that their prayers should be kingdom focused. Our prayers for our children should also be kingdom focused. I have developed this list of five things that I pray daily for my two girls. Feel free to use it if you would like or take some time to create your own.

1. I pray for their salvation. We, as parents, must realize that success and acceptance in this world should not be our goal for our children. That does not mean that these are wrong desires but your child's salvation must be priority number one! Everything you do as a parent should be focused on this priority – you first and foremost have a responsibility to proclaim both in word and deed the gospel.

---

60 Matthew 6:9-13

2. I pray that my girls will whole-heartedly follow God's call on their life. The mother of Samuel, Hannah, voiced a prayer to God that if He blessed her with a child then she would "give him to the Lord all the days of his life."[61] That is my attitude as well – God has blessed us and I, in turn, fully surrender my girls to His service whatever that may be.

3. I pray that they will be Great Commission Christians. Jesus' instructions to his disciples were to make disciples and my prayer is that my girls will do this. What an amazing blessing it would be to watch your child lead someone else to Christ!

4. I pray for their future mates. My mom modeled this for me and God answered her prayer. I ask God to bring a true helpmate into their lives at the right time, one that has a passionate personal relationship with Jesus Christ.

5. I pray that they will pass on a godly heritage to their children. My desire is to leave a legacy on this earth and I can think of no better way to do this than with my family. What will you pass on to your children that they will pass on to their children?

WHY ALL THE WORK?

Cultivating a gospel-centered home is not easy. In fact, it takes a lot of work and intentionality. There are moments in time in your child's life that will be ingrained in their memory forever. I remember certain family vacations with crystal clear clarity. I remember standing at the edge of the Grand Canyon amazed at the beauty of God's creation. I remember walking through the White House in Washington D.C. astounded that a single bedroom could be the same size as my entire house! But there are times in my life that stick out more than these great moments. I remember the hours of conversation with my parents, attending church together and watching God work in and through their lives. Your child will remember the ordinary rhythms of life and these moments will set the tone for his or her spiritual growth and development.

---

61 1 Samuel 1:11

If you ride through the country you will likely see old farm-houses with nothing remaining but the chimney. The entire structure of the house has deteriorated and is in shambles but the chimney continues to stand firm. I picture cultivating a gospel-centered home in this same way. Your child will see the "chimney" of a gospel-centered home even if they forget many of the other things in their childhood. There is an easy answer to why this is the case. The chimney continues to stand because it is part of the foundation of the house. In the same manner, when your child is saved, Jesus becomes the foundation of their life – "the chief cornerstone."[62] Our calling, as parents, is to faithfully point our children to Christ and build on that sure foundation.

---

62 Ephesians 2:20

5

FORGING A PARTNERSHIP: EQUIPPING PARENTS TO DISCIPLE THEIR CHILDREN

We have looked at the biblical responsibility parents have to disciple their children as well as some practical steps to take that will help cultivate a gospel-centered home. I want to continue this conversation by looking at the church's role in this process. If you are a pastor or ministry leader I encourage you to read this chapter with an open mind being completely honest concerning your church's successes and failures in this area. Parents, feel free to pass along this chapter to pastors and ministry leaders in your local church. Ultimately, my prayer is that a partnership will be forged between local church leaders and church members as they seek to impact the next generation with the gospel of Jesus Christ.

EVIDENCE OF THE PROBLEM

Evidence suggests that the church and its ministries have often overlooked the responsibility to equip parents to disciple their children. Steve Wright believes the church and family should work together to accomplish this but "a disconnect has formed over the past fifty years between the two institutions that were designed to work together."[63] Many children's and youth ministries have left parents out of the discipleship process and many parents have abdicated their responsibility to the church. Alvin Reid noted that a shift must take place in youth ministry "because the greatest impact in the life of youth is not made by their peers; the greatest impact in the life of youth is made by adults, and especially by parents."[64] There exists a need for the church and especially the children's and youth ministries to equip parents with the tools necessary to disciple their children.

THE RESPONSIBILITY TO EQUIP

Scripture indicates parents have the responsibility to disciple their children but the church also plays an important role in this task. Paul, in Ephesians 4:12, stated that leaders within the church should "equip the saints for the work of ministry, for building up the body of Christ." One of the fundamental roles of church leadership is to equip the body of Christ to do ministry. This is especially true with regard to equipping parents to fulfill the responsibility they have to be involved in the spiritual development of their children. Glenn Schultz wrote, "Church leaders must pay careful attention to the role they have in developing and supporting the home. Every effort needs to be made to strengthen the spiritual tenor of the family."[65] Ephesians 4:12 emphasizes that church leaders have a vital responsibility to equip parents to be involved actively in the spiritual development of their children.

One of the functions within the biblical role of church leadership is the responsibility to equip others. MacArthur explained this when he stated that pastor-teacher's should "provide the leadership and spiritual resources to cause believers to be taking on the likeness

---

63 Steve Wright, *Rethink: Is Student Ministry Working?* (Wake Forest, NC: InQuest Publishing, 2007), 106.

64 Reid, *Raising the Bar*, 154.

65 Glen Schultz, *Kingdom Education*, 2d ed. (Nashville: Lifeway Press, 2002), 95.

of their Lord and Savior through continual obedience to His Word and to provide a pattern, or example, of godliness (1 Thessalonians 1:2-7; 1 Peter 5:3)."[66] This is true with regard to equipping parents to train and disciple their children. Steve Wright noted, "We must accept the God-given role of parents as the primary discipler and position our ministry in a family-equipping role."[67] Pastors and ministry leaders should champion the family and the role parents have in the spiritual development of their children. This can be accomplished when pastors and church leaders provide resources that equip parents to take on their responsibility.

Several authors have recognized that youth ministry must focus its efforts on equipping parents to disciple their teenagers. Alvin Reid stated that "effective youth ministers will – instead of spending 90 percent of their time with students – spend perhaps a third of their time with the students, a third of the time with parents and other significant adults, and a third of the time with all of them together."[68] This will be a shift in mindset for many youth ministers but it will be the most effective way to transform the lives of teenagers. He insisted that youth ministers must spend time equipping parents to disciple their teenagers.

Mark DeVries also believes that youth ministry must recognize the importance of equipping parents to disciple their teenagers. He wrote, "Equipping parents for their work as the primary nurturers of their children's faith has been an essentially untapped resource in youth ministry."[69] This is alarming because of the biblical responsibility of parents and the influence they have in their teenager's spiritual formation. Effective youth ministries must seek to equip these parents for the task.

Steve Wright emphasized the need for churches to evaluate the way that youth ministry is accomplished. He noted that youth ministries must resource parents with the tools needed to be involved in the spiritual development of their teenager. He wrote, "Parents

66 MacArthur, *Ephesians*, 152.
67 Wright, *Rethink*, 86.
68 Reid, *Raising the Bar*, 154.
69 DeVries, *Family-Based Youth Ministry*, 104.

are resourced anytime they are given tools that allow them to guide, grow, train or encourage their child's faith development."[70] Youth ministries must partner with parents to help equip them as they disciple their teenagers.

Discipleship is a partnership between the parents and the church. Parents have the primary responsibility to disciple their children but the church also has a responsibility to equip parents to accomplish this task. I want to encourage pastors and ministry leaders to take a moment to take the following survey as they consider the church's role in equipping parents.

Instructions: Please fill in the blank with the number between 1 and 5 that most closely corresponds to your church's practice, using a scale of 1 to 5 with 1 = Not Very Often and 5 = Very Often.

1. How often are parents encouraged to be actively involved in their child's spiritual development? _____

2. How often do you provide resources to parents that encourage them to be actively involved in their child's spiritual development? _____

3. How often does your staff discuss how to equip parents to take an active role in their child's spiritual development? _____

4. How often does your church have events that include the entire family? _____

5. How often does your church/ministry assume the primary role for discipling children and teenagers? _____

---

70 Wright, *Rethink*, 158.

6. How often do your small group leaders emphasize and discuss parent's role and responsibility in the home?

    _____

7. How often does your staff pray for parents to step up and fulfill their biblical responsibility in the home?_____

    Circle the letter answer that most closely corresponds to your own practice.

1. In the course of a typical year, how often do you offer a specific training opportunity for parents?
    a) annually
    b) bi-annually
    c) quarterly
    d) monthly

2. In the course of a typical week, how much time does your children/student pastor spend with parents of kids in their ministry?
    a) none
    b) 0-15 minutes
    c) 15-30 minutes
    d) 30-45 minutes
    e) 45 minutes - 1 hour
    f) more than 1 hour

3. In the course of a typical year, how often does your primary preaching pastor emphasize the biblical role parents have to disciple their children?
    a) none
    b) weekly
    c) monthly
    d) quarterly
    e) bi-annually
    f) annually

Answer the following questions by circling True or False.

1. True / False   Parents know what their children are learning each week in church.

2. True / False   Our church provides specific parenting resources to help parents stay actively involved in their child's spiritual development.

3. True / False   Parents know what their biblical responsibility is in their home.

4. True / False   We encourage children and teenagers to discuss spiritual matters with their parents.

5. True / False   Parents are the primary influencer in a child's life.

6. True / False   Most of our parents have a plan for the spiritual development of their children.

7. True / False   Pastors should equip parents to disciple their children.

8. True / False   Our church has a strategy to equip parents to disciple their children.

9. True / False   Our church evaluates how involved our parents are in their child's spiritual development.

10. True / False   Our church offers a parenting class every year.

Please write your answers in the space provided.

1. Do you believe your church does a good job of equipping parents? Please explain your answer. _____
   _____
   _____
   _____
   _____
   _____

2. What is your church's strategy for helping parents take an active role in their child's spiritual development? Please explain your answer. _____
   _____
   _____
   _____
   _____
   _____

3. What is your church's greatest struggle as you think about equipping parents to disciple their children? Please explain your answer. _____
   _____
   _____
   _____
   _____
   _____

4. What steps can be taken to make equipping parents a priority in the life of your church? Please explain your answer. _____
   _____
   _____
   _____
   _____
   _____

The big question at this point is, how can pastors and ministry leaders help equip parents to fulfill this responsibility? It would be easy to say, "do these five things" but what follows are simply suggestions to consider as you look at equipping parents. Ultimately, churches need to develop a local church specific plan for equipping parents to disciple their children.

TRAINING

I enjoy working out and there have been times when I have utilized a personal trainer to help me develop a fitness plan. Each time I have used a trainer I have been able to accomplish things physically that I have not previously been able to accomplish. It's not that I don't know what I am doing in the gym but trainers are able to offer expertise that is beneficial. In the same way, pastors and ministry leaders can help equip parents through specific training.

One of the easiest ways to train parents to take a more active role in their child's spiritual development is through weekly preaching. I'm not suggesting that pastors should only preach on this topic but I do think we should take every opportunity to encourage our parents as biblical texts address their responsibility. I have sought to emphasize this consistently, especially during sermon application. It is necessary to remind parents of this vital role and responsibility as often as possible.

Another opportunity to equip parents is through small group opportunities. Working through a specific parenting study as well as tailoring discussion to address this vital responsibility can prove beneficial in helping parents understand their role and responsibility. It is also helpful when these small groups offer accountability and encouragement as parents seek to cultivate a gospel-centered home and disciple their children.

Churches should also consider hosting specific events to help train and equip parents to take their calling seriously. I have seen churches offer a parenting seminar during Vacation Bible School so that parents are equipped to take a more active role in their child's spiritual development. I would argue that effective children and student ministries engage and equip parents. Many times churches do a phenomenal job ministering to children and teenagers but they lose sight of the parents in this process.

RESOURCES

Historically, the church has encouraged parents to be involved in the spiritual development of their children and has offered resources to accomplish this task. One such resource that began to be used early in church history is the catechism. Tom Nettles emphasized that there is a lack of emphasis and even a sense of animosity towards catechisms in the church today. They were, however, of fundamental importance throughout much of church history. He wrote, "Such convictions may be held in all sincerity and may gain apparent support from selected facts, but suspicion of catechisms as a legitimate tool for teaching God's Word cannot be justified historically, biblically, or practically."[71] Nettles continued by emphasizing that catechisms were important throughout church history but specifically during the Reformation and in early Baptist life.

Voddie Baucham stated that parents should recover the use of catechisms as they seek to instruct their children. He wrote, "Through a series of questions and answers the child slowly learns what to believe and, more importantly, why."[72] This is important because it gives children the biblical foundation they desperately need. I have developed a list of 10 foundational principles that I believe are essential for parents to teach their children concerning the Christian faith and it is included as Appendix A in this book. Feel free to use it in your church and in your home.

Another key way to keep parents involved in the discipleship process is provide them with a handout that details what their children are learning each week. Many children's and youth curriculums have these resources available and, in our church, we have given them to parents when they pick their children up each week

71 Tom Nettles, "An Encouragement to Use Catechisms," *The Founders Journal* (Issue 10, Fall 1992), available from http://www.founders.org/journal/fj10/article3.html. Internet: accessed 21 March 2010.
72 Baucham, *Family-Driven Faith*, 119.

and encouraged them to discuss what kids have learned over Sunday lunch. I have also written a Christmas devotional for families to use during the month of December so that they can focus on Christ together. There are numerous resources like these that can be provided for parents as they seek to disciple their children and I would encourage churches to utilize them as often as possible.

REJECTING "SILO" MINISTRY

I believe one of the greatest struggles for the church today is the drift towards "silo" ministry and this has contributed to the lack of parental discipleship. By "silo" ministry I mean that many churches have so segregated children and youth ministries that they have become their own individual silos within the church. This is most clearly seen in youth ministry but it is growing to include children's ministry, as churches are placing more emphasis on this ministry area.

Recently, there has been increased interest in the responsibility that parents and the church have in the spiritual development of teenagers. This is largely due to the fact that there is a mass exodus of teens from the church after they graduate high school. Alvin Reid emphasized that ministry to teenagers must be evaluated and improved if the church hopes to reach the next generation. He stated that youth ministry can be a strong influence in a teenager's life "but the very best youth ministry should be nothing more for Christian families than an aid to them, providing a supporting, not a leading, role."[73] The youth ministry, therefore, should serve in a role that equips parents to disciple and train teenagers instead of taking that responsibility from them.

Voddie Baucham addressed this same topic from a different perspective. He agrees that the contemporary church should take a serious look at ministry to teenagers but insisted that the best approach is to do away with youth ministry all together. Baucham wrote, "Today parents are considered responsible if they find the church with the best-staffed nursery and the most up-to-date youth

---

73 Reid, *Raising the Bar*, 155.

ministry."[74] The problem with this approach is that God does not hold the youth ministry responsible for a child's spiritual development. Baucham insisted that a more biblical approach to ministry is a family-integrated model of church where there are no age-segregated ministries.[75]

Mark DeVries also emphasized that a shift needs to take place in contemporary youth ministry. He, unlike Baucham, insisted that youth ministry has its place in the church but it should be family-based. Youth ministries should recognize that their primary role is to empower parents and their secondary role is to equip the larger church family to minister to teenagers.[76] He stated that this approach to ministry can serve as the foundation for any type of youth ministry in any setting.

Steve Wright reported that the contemporary model for youth ministry has failed to prepare teenagers for life outside of youth ministry. The primary reason is that churches have failed to adequately equip parents to disciple their teenagers. He wrote, "Many churches are so busy running programs, filling slots and maintaining the outward veneer there isn't enough time left for strengthening families."[77] He feels churches should adopt a new strategy that equips families and the youth ministry should partner with parents. He insisted that this is the only way for churches to reverse the mass exodus of teenagers from the church.

Every pastor and ministry leader must take seriously their role to equip parents of children and teenagers if they hope to see the next generation reached with the gospel. I believe that training parents, resourcing them and rejecting "silo" ministry are all essential if we are going to see things change within the church. My prayer is that pastors and ministry leaders will catch this vision and we will see God do amazing things in our families and churches for his glory!

---

74 Baucham, *Family-Driven Faith*, 95.
75 Ibid., 177-183.
76 DeVries, *Family-Based Youth Ministry*, 103-105.
77 Wright, *ReThink*, 150-151.

LEGACY: CHANGING A GENERATION AND THE WORLD

I mentioned at the beginning of this book that my greatest hope and desire is to see Christian parents disciple their children and make a tremendous impact for God's kingdom in this world. Will you dream with me for just a second? Imagine what would happen if Christian parents understood their role and responsibility to be actively involved in their children's spiritual growth and actually took it seriously. Consider what would happen if these Christian parents were trained and resourced by pastors and ministry leaders with the tools necessary to disciple their children. What would be the result? Is it possible we could experience another Great Awakening? Would unreached people groups finally be reached with the gospel?

My fear is that many churches and parents are content with good kids instead of godly kids. Often, even Christian parents are satisfied with our kids chasing the American dream instead of chasing hard after Jesus. I believe we would see the church strengthened and the gospel spread throughout the world if we could catch the vision of parent-driven discipleship in our homes and churches.

Hope is not lost. I want to call our attention back in history when
God's people did and did not take this calling seriously and the
stunning results that followed.

JOSIAH

One of the more sobering events in the Bible, in my estimation, occurs in 2 Kings 22. At this point, the nation of Israel had
been divided into the northern kingdom (Jerusalem) and southern
kingdom (Judah). Things were not going well as we shall see. Josiah
assumed the throne at the age of eight, after his father Amon was
assassinated. At the age of eighteen, he decided to begin rebuilding
the temple. The people of Judah had walked away from the Lord
and were worshiping a number of other gods but Josiah began
seeking the Lord.

As the construction project began, word came quickly to Josiah that a book had been found. That book was the Law of God
(likely the first five books of the Bible). Yes, God's people had lost
the Bible for years! Josiah asked for the book to be read and as soon
as he heard God's law he tore his clothes. He said, "Go inquire of
the Lord for me, and for the people, and for all Judah, concerning
the words of this book that has been found. For great is the wrath
of the Lord that is kindled against us, because our fathers have
not obeyed the words of this book, to do according to all that is
written concerning us."[78] Josiah was terrified. He knew that God's
judgment would soon fall because his people were not remaining
faithful to the covenant he had established with them.

So, what did Josiah do? How did he respond? 2 Kings 23:1-3
describes the story in vivid detail, "Then the king sent, and all the
elders of Judah and Jerusalem were gathered to him. And the king
went up to the house of the Lord, and with him all the men of
Judah and all the inhabitants of Jerusalem and the priests and the
prophets, all the people, both small and great. And he read in their
hearing all the words of the Book of the Covenant that had been
found in the house of the Lord. And the king stood by the pillar

---

78 2 Kings 22:13

and made a covenant before the Lord, to walk after the Lord and to keep his commandments and his testimonies and his statutes with all his heart and all his soul, to perform the words of this covenant that were written in this book. And all the people joined in the covenant." The scene was reminiscent of what happened between God and his people at various points in the Old Testament. Josiah led God's people to recommit themselves to follow his law and teach it to their children.

I wish that I could say that the people in Judah continued upholding this covenant with God and passed it along to their children and grandchildren. They did not. In fact, shortly after Josiah's death King Nebuchadnezzar and the Babylonian empire overtook God's people in Judah and led them into captivity. I wonder what would have happened if God's people had taken his covenant seriously and diligently discipled their children. Could judgment have been done away with and God's blessing and favor showered on his people?

DANIEL & HIS FRIENDS

One of my favorite characters in the entire Bible is Daniel and his story actually picks up shortly after Josiah. I am amazed at his confidence in the Lord in the face of difficult circumstances and how God used him in a powerful way. Daniel's story does not begin with much promise. In fact, Daniel was a young man when God's judgment fell upon the nation of Israel as the Babylonian king Nebuchadnezzar besieged the city of Jerusalem. The king determined to gather the best and brightest young men in Jerusalem and indoctrinate them in Chaldean culture and knowledge. The logic was clear: If the king could wipe away any trace of Jewish heritage or belief among the future leaders of Israel then he could be assured that he would never have to fear a revolt.

The king only had one problem, a major problem. Daniel and his friends, Hananiah, Mishael, and Azariah (also known as Shadrach, Meshach, and Abed-Nego) had been taught God's law as children. Even though the nation of Israel was experiencing God's judgment for unfaithfulness to his covenant, it is evident that discipleship in the home as commanded by God in Deuteronomy 6 had been carried out with these young men. We know this because of their response to the king's commands in Daniel 1:8, "But Daniel purposed in his heart that he would not defile himself with the portion of the king's delicacies, nor with the wine which he drank; therefore he requested of the chief of the eunuchs that he might not defile himself." These young men refused to compromise their convictions.

The story does not end there. In Daniel 3, we see another time when Daniel's friends had to choose to remain faithful to the God of Israel or face death. King Nebuchadnezzar had golden idol made in the likeness of himself and required everyone to bow down and worship the statue or be thrown into a fiery furnace. David's friends refused. "Shadrach, Meshach, and Abed-Nego answered and said to the king, 'O Nebuchadnezzar, we have no need to answer you in this matter. If this be so, our God whom we serve is able to deliver us from the burning fiery furnace, and he will deliver us out of your hand, O king. But if not, be it known to you, O king, that we will not serve your gods or worship the golden image that you have set up."[79] Once again, these young men refused to compromise their convictions even in the face of death.

We see a final picture of Daniel's resolve to serve the Lord in Daniel 6. At this point, Daniel had risen to a position of prominence in the Babylonian kingdom to the point that the current king had considered making him second in command. The other officials were not pleased with this decision and decided to exploit his devotion to God so that they could get him into trouble. They convinced the king to declare that no one in the kingdom could pray to another god besides the king for thirty days. Daniel refused to obey this law and was punished by being thrown into a den of lions. The Lord sustained him and protected his life during this ordeal and, as a result, the king declared that Daniel's God was the one true and living God that should be worshiped.

---

79 Daniel 3:16-18

The book of Daniel records a remarkable transformation in the Babylonian kingdom because a few young men stood strong for the Lord in the midst of difficulties. They refused to yield to the authority of a pagan king because they were committed to upholding the law of God. As a result of their faithfulness, an entire nation, far from the one true God, was able to see his power and faithfulness. What would have happened if Daniel and his friends were not taught the law of God when they were young? What if Daniel, Shadrach, Meshach and Abed-Nego's parents had abdicated this responsibility to someone else?

The First Great Awakening

I majored in history in college and one of my favorite subjects to study is the First Great Awakening in the United States. When you drill down deep into what happened during this period you quickly recognize that the First Great Awakening demonstrated the great impact young people are able to make on culture. Alvin Reid wrote, "Recall that Jonathan Edwards recorded on more than one occasion that the First Great Awakening was, more than anything, a youth movement."[80] Reid also emphasized that youth have served as the catalyst for many of the religious awakenings that have occurred throughout the world since the First Great Awakening.[81]

After watching God move in a powerful way throughout the American colonies, Jonathan Edwards wrote, "Ever since the great work of God that was wrought here about nine years ago, there has been a great abiding alteration in this town in many respects. There has been vastly more religion kept up in the town, among all sorts of persons, in religious exercises and in common conversation than used to be before. There has remained a more general seriousness and decency in attending the public worship. There has been a very great alteration among the youth of the town with respect to reveling, frolicking, profane and unclean conversation, and lewd songs. Instances of fornication have been very rare. There has also

---

80 Reid, *Raising the Bar*, 65.
81 Ibid., 65-71.

been a great alteration among both old and young with respect to tavern haunting. I suppose the town has been in no measure so free of vice in these respects for any long time together for this sixty years as it has been this nine years past."[82] Did you catch that? The greatest catalysts for revival in Jonathan Edward's mind were the young people. What would have happened if these young people were not discipled? Would the Great Awakening have happened?

WHAT WILL BE OUR LEGACY?

If we are going to make an impact in this world and leave a gospel legacy we need to focus on this generation. Parents and churches must partner together to accomplish this mission. I have talked with many people concerned about the state of our country. If trends continue, fewer people will be involved in church next year and fewer people will have a biblical worldview. The reality is that we can wring our hands and live in fear of the future or we can take a stand and focus on the next generation. I believe the battle will be won or lost in our homes. Will we, as Christian parents, commit to raise up an entire generation of young people that know Jesus and want to make him known? Will churches take seriously their role to equip parents to accomplish this task?

I want to encourage you to take a few moments and spend time in prayer. If you are a parent I encourage you to ask God to burden your heart with the desire to take an active role in your child's spiritual development. Ask him to give you wisdom as you seek to cultivate a gospel-centered home and pass on a godly heritage to your children and grandchildren. If you are a pastor or ministry leader I encourage you to ask God to give you a clear vision and strategy for equipping parents in your church as they fulfill their God-given responsibility in the home. Finally, ask God to raise up a generation of Daniels who are willing to stand for the truth as they make a tremendous impact for the cause of the gospel of Jesus Christ.

---

82 http://www.nhinet.org/ccs/docs/awaken.htm

FULL DISCLOSURE: ANSWERING COMMON QUESTIONS AND CONCERNS

I hope that this book has challenged you regardless of whether you are a parent or church leader. As I have shared my ideas about parent-driven discipleship and the role parents and churches play with others, I have met some resistance. In this final chapter, my goal is to address some of the common questions and concerns that are often raised. First, I want to address some concerns parents have shared with me and then I want to discuss some concerns church leaders have shared with me regarding parent-driven discipleship.

PARENT CONCERNS

Concern #1:

"If I do everything you say can I be assured that my child will not walk away from the Lord? After all the Bible says to train up a child in the way he should go and when he is old he will not depart." This verse is one that must be explained because of its apparent implications. It seems as though this verse gives assurance that if you raise your child in the ways of the Lord then they will continue in the ways of the Lord for the remainder of their life no matter what. If you take one look at the children who have come through the church you might dismiss this verse as a hopeful thought but not reality.

First, I want to approach this discussion with a great deal of caution and understanding. I personally know a godly man whose son is far from living a godly life. This man, to my knowledge, has sought to raise his child in the love and admonition of the Lord Jesus Christ, yet his son continues to rebel. We must not look at this verse in Proverbs and come to the conclusion that it is an untrue statement. The book of Proverbs must be interpreted in a proper manner. We must realize that these proverbs are not the same as covenants or promises. God made a covenant with his people that he would bless them if they kept his commandments. This is not a negotiable promise – God will keep his word in relation to the people's obedience. But a proverb is different than a covenant or promise. The better way to understand this verse is that in most situations if you train your children in the way they should go, they will continue walking in that way.

There comes a point where your children are no longer under your jurisdiction. God holds parents accountable for the way they raise their children but we must also recognize that God holds people individually accountable for their actions and their choices. Does this mean that parents are let off the hook completely? Absolutely not! You have a responsibility to raise your children rightly but your children are also held responsible before God for their choices. I do want to set forth a challenge in light of this discussion. I believe the pendulum can swing too far on each side of this issue. Parents can totally wash their hands in relation to their children and they can also dwell on the fact that they must have done something wrong because their children have strayed away from the Lord. We must not swing the pendulum too far! I honestly believe that we have dropped the ball in regards to teaching our children the ways of the Lord. We have made excuses, failed to set aside the time and filled our plates with too many other "important" things to do.

It will not matter in eternity whether or not your child made straight A's, whether or not they played college or professional athletics, or whether or not they were successful and prosperous according to the world's standards. It will matter immensely whether or not your child comes to a saving knowledge of Jesus Christ and you have an amazing opportunity, as a parent, to share the gospel with them daily and purposefully!

Concern #2:

"I should leave the spiritual development of my children to the experts. After all, I don't have a degree in theology or any experience in teaching the Bible." Some parents insist that professionally trained "experts" should take the primary role in the spiritual development of their children. Barna emphasized that American society enables parents to rely on "institutions such as schools, community organizations, churches, the mass media, and government agencies to pick up the slack and cover for parents while they are trying to change the world in their nine-to-five roles."[83] He also wrote that parents should take the leadership role with their children because "leaving the job to the religious professionals is an inappropriate transfer of authority and power to people and organizations that God never intended."[84] Many parents, however, insist that these experts are better equipped to train their children with regards to spiritual matters.

Voddie Baucham believes that parents abdicate their responsibility because of the current age of professionalism. He noted that parents spare no expense to make sure that their children will succeed in whatever area they desire.[85] Steve Wright stated that parents and churches often view youth ministry as a "spiritual drop-

---

83 Barna, *Revolutionary Parenting*, 28.
84 Ibid, 96.
85 Baucham, *Family Driven Faith*, 93.

off service best left to the professionals."[86] This causes parents to take on the responsibility of merely placing the teenager in a spiritual environment instead of taking an active role in their spiritual development.[87] When parents believe experts are responsible for their child's spiritual development, they remove themselves from this position. Pastors and ministry leaders do have specific training and experience that can be helpful as parents fulfill their God-given responsibility. In fact, I think parents would be wise to avail themselves of any help and guidance that pastors can provide. However, parents must recognize that the primary responsibility falls to them.

Concern #3:

"I know I have a biblical responsibility to be involved in my child's spiritual life but I do not have much influence." Many parents believe they have no influence in their child's life when it comes to spiritual matters, especially as their children become teenagers. Christian Smith stated, "Parents are normally very important in shaping the religious and spiritual lives of their teenage children even though they may not realize it.'[88] Even though parents do not believe they have much influence, Barna insisted, "More than three out of four teenagers (78 percent) acknowledge that their parents have a lot of impact on their thoughts and deeds."[89] Regardless of these statistics, some parents continue to insist that they have little influence in the lives of their teenagers.

Steve Wright discussed this matter and noted that the contemporary culture gives evidence that parents have a great influence on their teenagers. He cited examples from publications sponsored by Anheuser-Busch, Coors Brewing Company, MTV and the Associated Press, and USA Today Weekend Magazine.[90] Each publication

---

86 Wright, *Rethink*, 47.
87 Ibid.
88 Smith, *Soul Searching*, 56.
89 George Barna, *Real Teens: A Contemporary Snapshot of Youth Culture* (Ventura, CA: Regal Books, 2001), 72.
90 Wright, *Rethink*, 81-83.

encouraged parents to talk to their teenagers about issues that matter because they are the greatest influence in their teenagers' lives.

Mark DeVries emphasized that parental involvement or lack thereof influences decisions made by teenagers. Positive decisions are a direct result of parental involvement and negative decisions stem from a lack of parental involvement. This is especially true with regards to the spiritual development of teenagers.[91] Parents have a tremendous amount on influence regardless of whether their children are toddlers or teenagers.

Concern #4:

"I do not want to fail spiritually and my child think I am a hypocrite." Most children recognize whether or not their parents have a growing relationship with Jesus Christ. Parents understand this and many struggle to be involved in the spiritual development of their children because they do not want to make any mistakes or appear fake. Ray Comfort noted that parents influence their children in numerous ways but the greatest influence will be the parents' "own personal example of how to live the Christian life."[92] Mark DeVries emphasized that many Christian parents are not spiritually mature and this has negatively affected the spiritual development of children.[93]

Baucham recognized this concern and stated, "If you can read, you can teach your children God's Word."[94] He continued by encouraging parents to trust that God will guide them as they seek to faithfully guide their children. Dennis Rainey noted that it is difficult to be a consistent follower of Christ at home. He wrote, "When you are at home, surrounded by a mate who knows you well and several little disciples who are intently observing your ev-

---

91 DeVries, *Family-Based Youth Ministry*, 62-65.
92 Ray Comfort, *How to Bring Your Children to Christ … & Keep Them There: Avoiding the Tragedy of False Conversion* (Genesis Publishing Group, 2005), 163.
93 DeVries, *Family-Based Youth Ministry*, 73.
94 Baucham, *Family-Driven Faith*, 93.

ery word and move, it's hard to keep up a front for long."[95] Rainey concluded by emphasizing that parents need to consistently live out a vital relationship with Jesus Christ and trust that God will take care of everything else.[96]

One of the most memorable moments in my parenting life to date was when I had to ask my daughter for her forgiveness. Our children need to see that we need God's grace and forgiveness just as much as them. After I had lost my temper with her I went to her and apologized. I shared that daddy still struggles with sin and needs Jesus just like she does. My daughter looked at me and said, "Daddy, that was the best 'I'm sorry' I have ever heard!" We do not have to be perfect parents because we serve a perfect Savior.

Concern #5:

"My primary concern is that my child stay out of trouble. As long as he or she does that everything must be ok." Some parents equate regulating a child's behavior with being involved in their spiritual development. Paul Tripp wrote, concerning parents, "They fear the big three vices of the teen years: drugs and alcohol, sex, and dropping out of school."[97] He noted, however, that parents should recognize behavior is merely a window into the heart. They should address the sinful desires of the heart, which requires them to be involved actively in their child's spiritual development.[98]

The inherent problem with this is that parents are not deeply involved in their child's life. Parents merely observe the behavior of their children and never move beyond appearance to the person their child is becoming. Ron Luce stated that parents spend little time in meaningful conversation with their children while these same children are bombarded with hours upon hours of media driven values.[99] The only hint that a problem exists with their teenager

---

95 Rainey, *Growing a Spiritually Strong Family*, 17.
96 Ibid.
97 Tripp, *Age of Opportunity*, 110.
98 Tripp, *Age of Opportunity*, 110-113.
99 Luce, *Recreate*, 58-60.

is when he or she begins to rebel. Parents who are involved actively in the spiritual development of their children will be able to gauge their child's spiritual health by more than just behavior.

CHURCH LEADER CONCERNS

Concern #1:

"What do you do with kids whose parents are not actively involved in church or may not even be believers?" This is probably the question I hear most often from pastors and ministry leaders. Let me say, first, this is a great "problem" to have. The reality that we have children and teenagers in our church is a blessing regardless of their individual circumstances. However, we must meet them where they are, share the gospel with them and disciple them.

So, how do you do that as a church when parents are not involved? Let me tell you a story about my best friend in high school, Matt. He was a great guy and we played baseball and football together. Matt's parents were not involved in a church at all during his high school years and, due to our friendship, my parents essentially adopted him spiritually. He went to church with us each week and my parents invested in him as if he were their son. After we graduated high school and moved away to separate colleges, Matt walked through some difficult circumstances. The first person he called during this time was my dad. Not long after that, Matt's parents began attending church with my parents and remain actively involved in church to this day.

I think this personal story gives us a bit of perspective when we look at children and teenagers whose parents are not involved in church. The reality is that they will not be discipled in their home. But that does not mean that they cannot be discipled by someone. My encouragement to pastors and church ministry leaders is to identify families who are doing this well and encourage them to "spiritually adopt" children and teenagers whose parents are not actively involved in church. James 1:27 reminds us that pure religion is to take care of the orphans and widows who are suffering. The immediate application of this verse is meeting physical needs but I believe it can be extended to spiritual needs. There are children and teenagers in our churches that are spiritual orphans and we must take care to see that someone steps in on their behalf.

Concern #2:

"What do you do with parents in the church who will not take an active role in their child's spiritual development regardless of what you do?" I must confess that this is one of the greatest struggles I have had as a pastor and youth pastor. There are many Christian parents that go to extremes to be actively involved in their kid's lives in every area but their spiritual life. Many have the mindset that if their children are at church on a semi-regular basis they will grow spiritually.

First, I would encourage you to pray for these parents and ask that God would grab a hold of their heart and help them understand how vital it is for them to fulfill their God-given role in this area. Regardless of how well we preach about this issue and emphasize it in our churches, God must do the heart work in parent's lives. Second, spend time with parents on a personal basis and encourage them in this area. It is one thing to preach and teach about this responsibility but I have found that addressing this in the context of a personal relationship with a parent goes a long way.

Some Christian parents are not going to take an active role in their child's spiritual growth and development regardless of what we do. We must recognize this and not take it personally. I do think we can approach these situations in much the same way as we do children whose parents are not involved in the church. We can find other godly men and women who can step in and help disciple these children and teenagers.

Concern #3:

"We have tried to incorporate the children's and youth ministries into the rest of the church but it is extremely difficult." I remember being a youth pastor and attempting to incorporate some of my teenagers into a church wide Bible study (previously we had done our own "youth" study separate from everyone else). This was one of the most awkward experiences and I realized quickly that the parents and teenagers involved in my ministry were not accustomed to spending time together like this. In fact, this was one of the defining moments as I considered how to encourage and equip parents to interact with their teenagers on a spiritual level. This is not an easy task and it takes time.

I would encourage pastors and ministry leaders to take a three-fold approach. First, teach what has been outlined in this book: parents should be actively involved in their child's spiritual growth and development. Many parents simply do not know that they have this responsibility. Second, create non-teaching environments when parents and children/teenagers can just be together. When I was a youth pastor, we had specific events throughout the year that served the purpose of letting teenagers and parents spend time together hanging out. I was amazed at how these times strengthened the families and opened doors for conversation down the road. Third, don't give up. Press on!

An Open Invitation

I am sure that there are other concerns and questions you may have after reading this book. Feel free to get in touch with me as you work through the ideas and concepts presented. I am by no means an expert but I am confident that parents and churches need to partner together to disciple the next generation. Join with me in praying that others would catch this vision and the gospel would go forth in power.

APPENDIX A

10 FOUNDATIONAL PRINCIPLES FOR CHILDREN

I thought it would be helpful to provide parents a place to start as they begin talking with their children about the things of the Lord. I believe there are some foundational principles concerning the Christian faith that every parent should teach their children. The questions and answers that follow are not exhaustive but I do believe they will help children gain a better understanding of the major truths of Scripture. Our calling, as parents, is to raise our children in the nurture and admonition of the Lord and my prayer is that this will be helpful as you seek to fulfill this calling.

1. What is the Bible and what is it about?

The Bible is one large book comprised of 66 individual books and grouped together into the Old and New Testaments. It is the Word of God delivered through human authors over the span of about 1,500 years. Paul wrote, in 2 Timothy 3:16-17, "All Scripture is breathed out by God and profitable for teaching, for reproof, for correction, and for training in righteousness, that the man of God may be complete, equipped for every good work."

At its core the Bible is a story…a love story. This love story is comprised of 4 scenes: Creation, Fall, Redemption and Restoration. In the first scene, Creation, we see that God created everything that exists. He created the sun and the moon, the trees and the grass, the fish and the birds, and even mankind. God's desire was that his creation would love and glorify him. Adam and Eve, the first human beings walked with God and he told them how they could love and obey him (Genesis 1-2).

In the second scene, Fall, we witness Adam and Eve rebelling against God by disobeying his Word (Genesis 3). As a result, they attempted to hide from him and the relationship they enjoyed with God was broken because of their sin. God did not leave Adam and Eve alone in their sin and he made them a very special promise. He told them that he would send someone to rescue them and all mankind from sin and make it possible for us to once again have a relationship with God. The remainder of the Old Testament emphasizes God's love for his people and their longing for the rescuer to come (Genesis 4 – Malachi).

In the third scene, Redemption, we encounter this rescuer sent by God (Matthew – 3 John). His name is Jesus and he is God's only Son. Jesus lived a perfect life and gave his life for us on the cross so that we would be able to have a relationship with God. We are called to place our faith and trust in him for salvation. After his resurrection, Jesus told his followers to preach the gospel all over the world and make disciples until his return. This is the mission of every believer and every church.

In the fourth and final scene, Restoration, Jesus returns to set all things right and establish his kingdom on earth (Revelation). In this new kingdom, Jesus rules in righteousness, and all believers enjoy his presence for all eternity. There will be no sorrow or sickness, no sin or pain, and no death. It will be perfect!

2. Who is God and what is He like?

The Bible tells us that God is one in essence and three in persons. We call this the Trinity. God has always existed in three distinct persons: Father, Son and Holy Spirit. This is a bit confusing but it is what the Scripture teaches. It may be helpful to think about it this way: the Father is God, the Son is God, the Holy Spirit is God but they are not three separate Gods; they are only one God… one in essence and three in persons.

God the Father rules over his creation with great care and concern. All of creation displays his glory and magnifies his name throughout the world. He loved mankind so much that he willingly sent his only Son to the world to give his life so that we may have eternal life (John 3:16). All who trust in Jesus for salvation enjoy the privilege of being called sons and daughters of God the Father.

God the Son, having eternally existed, came to this earth in what we call the Incarnation. He was conceived of the Holy Spirit and born of Mary, a virgin. Jesus lived a perfectly sinless life, died on the cross for our sins, was buried and rose from the dead on the third day (1 Corinthians 15:1-4). If we place our faith and trust in him we will receive God's free gift of salvation.

God the Holy Spirit is the third member of the Trinity and inspired men to write the Scriptures. He also enables us to understand the Scriptures when we read them and helps convict us of sin. We are baptized into the Holy Spirit at the moment of salvation; he dwells within the believer and gives each of us a spiritual gift to be used to build up the body of Christ.

3. Why did God create mankind?

God did not create mankind because he was lonely; he was in perfect relationship with himself as the Trinity – Father, Son, and Holy Spirit. We were created to have a relationship with God, to worship him and to glorify him in everything that we do in life. When God created Adam and Eve, he walked with them in the garden and they were able to enjoy his presence. The greatest longing of every human heart is to have a relationship with God.

Blaise Pascal said, "There is a God shaped vacuum in the heart of every man which cannot be filled by any created thing, but only by God, the Creator, made known through Jesus."

Psalm 19 reminds us that all of God's creation proclaims his glory every second of every day but this is not always true of mankind. God desires to have a relationship with us and he also gives us the freedom to choose to worship and glorify him or not. He does not force us to love and worship him. We have a choice and it is a choice every single person must make individually.

4.   What is sin and why does it matter?

In Genesis 3, we encounter sin for the very first time. After God created Adam, he told him that he could eat the fruit from every tree in the garden except the tree in the middle of the garden, the tree of the knowledge of good and evil. Adam and Eve chose to disobey God and they ate the fruit from this tree. In that instant their relationship with God was broken and they immediately tried to hide from him. That is exactly what sin does; it brings shame and separates us from our heavenly Father.

Sin has been described as "missing the mark" in the same way that an arrow misses the bull's-eye on a target. The bull's-eye is God's perfect standard and when we fail to hit that standard, we sin. Paul, in Romans 3:23, wrote, "For all have sinned and fall short of the glory of God." That includes you and me.

The reason sin is such a big deal is that God is holy and he cannot be around sin. For us to have a relationship with a holy God, we need to be without sin. The problem is that we are born sinners and unless we are forgiven of our sins we cannot have a relationship with God. This is exactly why Jesus died on the cross… to forgive us of our sins and enable us to have a relationship with our heavenly father.

5. What are the 10 Commandments and why are they important?

God gave the 10 Commandments to his people, Israel, shortly after they left Egypt. These commandments show God's character and they give guidance for how his people should live in this world. Here are the 10 Commandments:

1. I am the LORD your God; you shall have no other gods before me.
2. You shall not make for yourself an idol. You shall not bow down to them or worship them for I am a jealous God.
3. You shall not make wrongful use of the name of the LORD your God.
4. Remember the Sabbath day and keep it holy.
5. Honor your father and mother.
6. You shall not murder.
7. You shall not commit adultery.
8. You shall not steal.
9. You shall not bear false witness against your neighbor.
10. You shall not covet your neighbor's home, wife, or anything that belongs to your neighbor.

Jesus summed up the 10 Commandments in Matthew 22:37-40 when he said, "You shall love the Lord your God with all your heart and with all your soul and with all your mind. This is the great and first commandment. And a second is like it: You shall love your neighbor as yourself. On these two commandments depend all the Law and the Prophets." As you can see, Jesus divided the 10 Commandments into two sections: Commandments 1-4 emphasize our relationship with God and Commandments 6-10 emphasize our relationship with one another.

Ultimately, the 10 Commandments show us that we need a Savior. Paul said that the commandments function like a mirror to show us our sinfulness. It is impossible for us to keep the commandments perfectly, which is why we desperately need Jesus. He was the only one who perfectly kept all of God's commandments which means he was the only one who could serve as a sacrifice for our sin.

6.   What is the gospel and why is it important?

The gospel, at its core, is good news. It is the good news that Jesus left heaven and came to this earth to give his life as a sacrifice for our sins. He took your place and my place on the cross and received God's wrath against sin on himself so that we would be able to have a relationship with our heavenly father.

Jesus not only came to this earth and died, but he also rose from the dead. In rising from the dead, Jesus proved that our sin debt was fully paid and that death could not hold him. When we place our faith and trust in Jesus for salvation we participate in his death, burial and resurrection (demonstrated in baptism – Romans 6:4).

The gospel is important because it is the greatest news that could ever be proclaimed and it is where true hope can be found. It is the message that transforms our lives and gives true meaning as we live in this world.

7.   What is salvation?

When we talk about salvation we are primarily talking about being saved from our sins and receiving eternal life. This is summed up well in some familiar verses, "For God so loved the world, that he gave his only Son, that whoever believes in him should not perish but have eternal life. For God did not send his Son into the world to condemn the world, but in order that the world might be saved through him" (John 3:16-17).

It is important to recognize that the Bible emphasizes three distinct aspects of salvation: (1) justification, (2) sanctification and (3) glorification. Justification is the term used to describe what happens the moment we are saved. When we place our faith and trust in Jesus for salvation we are declared righteous by God the Father. We are not righteous because of what we have done but because of what

Jesus has done on our behalf. When God the Father looks at us, he sees Christ's righteousness covering our sin (Romans 4:23-24).

Sanctification describes our growth in the Christian life (1 Thessalonians 4:1-8). The word, sanctify, means to "set apart" and as we grow in the Christian life we begin to look more and more like Jesus (Romans 8:29). This is not a matter of us working for our salvation but allowing the Holy Spirit to work in and through us to make us more holy. As Christians, we are called to be "in the world but not of the world" meaning that, if we are saved, there should be something different about our lives.

The last aspect of salvation is called glorification and describes what happens when we die as a Christian. It is the culmination of the process of salvation when we enter the presence of God perfectly righteous and complete in Christ.

8. What is a disciple?

Simply put a disciple is a follower of Jesus. When Jesus left this earth, he gave his followers a commission: "Go therefore and make disciples of all nations, baptizing them in the name of the Father and of the Son and of the Holy Spirit, teaching them to observe all that I commanded you. And behold, I am with you always, to the end of the age."

First, a disciple is someone who responds to the gospel message and receives the free gift of salvation that has been offered by God. Second, a disciple is committed to living a life of obedience, which begins by following Jesus' command to be baptized in the name of the Father, Son and Holy Spirit. Baptism is an outward symbol of the inward change in a person's life and should be the first step of Christian obedience. Third, a disciple is a student of the Scriptures. He or she studies God's Word and allows it to serve as a foundation for a life of godliness.

Following Jesus is costly and he summed it up best when he told the crowd, "If anyone would come after me, let him deny himself and take up his cross daily and follow me" (Luke 9:23).

9. What is the "Fruit of the Spirit?"

When a person places his or her faith and trust in Jesus for salvation, the Holy Spirit comes to dwell within every Christian. His purpose is to lead and guide believers towards maturity in the faith and to be set apart for His purposes. Paul, in Galatians 5:16-25, reminds us that we will produce fruit as we yield to the Holy Spirit's work in our lives. Here is the fruit that he says should be present in the life of a Christian:

1. Love
2. Joy
3. Peace
4. Patience
5. Kindness
6. Generosity
7. Faithfulness
8. Gentleness
9. Self-Control

But how is that fruit produced? Jesus had a lot to say about bearing fruit in John 15. He said, "Abide in me, and I in you. As the branch cannot bear fruit by itself, unless it abides in the vine, neither can you, unless you abide in me. I am the vine; you are the branches. Whoever abides in me and I in him, he it is that bears much fruit, from apart from me you can do nothing." We bear fruit as we abide in a close relationship with Jesus Christ. This close relationship is marked by obedience to his Word.

10. Why should I read the Bible and pray?

When we talk about having a relationship with God we must recognize that it is similar to any other relationship in that it must be cultivated. We develop relationships with others by spending time with them and conversing with them. The same is true with our relationship with God. It must be cultivated and this happens through deep, intimate conversation with him. How, you ask? We do this primarily through spending time reading His Word and in prayer.

When we read the Bible we are entering into a conversation with God. He has spoken to us in His Word. As we read and study the Scriptures, the Holy Spirit works to illumine the text so that we see and understand what God is saying. We are not reading some old, dusty book but one that is living and active (Hebrews 4:12).

Prayer is the other way we commune with God. Our primary aim in prayer is not to get God to do something for us but to yield to how he is already at work around us in the world. Jesus modeled beautify how our prayers should look when he said, in the garden of Gethsemane, "not as I will, but as you will" (Matthew 26:39).

It is important for children to see the value of Scripture and I encourage parents to read to children even when they are very young. You can begin with something like the *Jesus Storybook Bible* and move to easier books of the Bible like 1 John when they learn to read in school. As children get older, especially in their teenage years, I would encourage parents to get them a good study Bible and load them up with good Bible studies (*Energion* produces a number of book studies that are helpful in this regard).

APPENDIX B

PARENTS QUESTIONNAIRE

Instructions: Please fill in the blank with the number of the answer that most closely corresponds to your own practice, using a scale of 1 to 5, with 1 = Not Involved and 5 = Very Involved

1. How involved would you say you are in your child's spiritual development? _____

2. How often do you read the Bible together with your family on a weekly basis? _____

3. How often do you pray together with your family on a weekly basis, excluding mealtimes? _____

4. How often does your child come to talk to you about spiritual matters on a weekly basis? _____

5. How often do you sit down together at the table to eat (breakfast, lunch, or dinner) on a weekly basis? _____

6. How often do you discuss cultural issues with your child (i.e. news, movies, books, etc.)? _____

7. How often do you pray for your child on a weekly basis? _____

Circle the letter answer that most closely corresponds to your own practice.

1. In the course of a typical week, how often do you spend in Bible study and prayer?
    a) daily
    b) a couple of times a week
    c) once a week
    d) never

2. In the course of a typical week, how much television do you watch?
    a) 1-5 hours
    b) 5-10 hours
    c) 10-15 hours
    d) 15-20 hours
    e) more than 20 hours
    f) I do not watch television

3. In the course of a typical week, how much time do you spend with your child/children?
    a) 1-5 hours
    b) 5-10 hours
    c) 10-15 hours
    d) 15-20 hours
    e) more than 20 hours

Answer the following questions by circling True or False.

1. True / False   Absolute moral truth exists.

2. True / False   Jesus Christ lived a sinless life during his earthly ministry.

3. True / False   God created the universe and continues to rule it today.

4. True / False   Salvation can be earned by good works.

5. True / False   The Bible contains some errors.

6. True / False   The Bible teaches the doctrine of the Trinity.

7. True / False   Jesus Christ was born of a virgin.

8. True / False   Miracles recorded in the Bible are not true.

9. True / False   Christians should share the gospel with non-believers.

10. True / False   Satan is not a real living entity.

Please write your answers in the space provided.

1. What are your goals for your child/children? _____
_____
_____
_____
_____
_____
_____

2. Do you have a plan for being involved in your child's/children's spiritual development? Please explain your answer. _____

_____

_____

_____

_____

_____

_____

3. Do you believe your child/children has/have a biblical worldview? Please explain your answer. _____

_____

_____

_____

_____

_____

_____

4. What are some biblical references that specifically discuss the relationship between parents and children? _____

_____

_____

_____

_____

_____

_____

5. What do you think should be the type of relationship between Christian parents and the church? _____

_____

_____

_____

_____

_____

APPENDIX

C

CHURCH QUESTIONNAIRE

Instructions: Please fill in the blank with the number between 1 and 5 that most closely corresponds to your church's practice, using a scale of 1 to 5 with 1 = Not Very Often and 5 = Very Often.

1. How often are parents encouraged to be actively involved in their child's spiritual development? _____

2. How often do you provide resources to parents that encourage them to be actively involved in their child's spiritual development? _____

3. How often does your staff discuss how to equip parents to take an active role in their child's spiritual development?

_____

4. How often does your church have events that include the entire family? _____

5. How often does your church/ministry assume the primary role for discipling children and teenagers? _____

6. How often do your small group leaders emphasize and discuss parent's role and responsibility in the home? _____

7. How often does your staff pray for parents to step up and fulfill their biblical responsibility in the home? _____

Circle the letter answer that most closely corresponds to your own practice.

1. In the course of a typical year, how often do you offer a specific training opportunity for parents?
    a) annually
    b) bi-annually
    c) quarterly
    d) monthly

2. In the course of a typical week, how much time does your children/student pastor spend with parents of kids in their ministry?
    a) none
    b) 0-15 minutes
    c) 15-30 minutes
    d) 30-45 minutes
    e) 45 minutes - 1 hour
    f) more than 1 hour

3. In the course of a typical year, how often does your primary preaching pastor emphasize the biblical role parents have to disciple their children?
    a) none
    b) weekly
    c) monthly

    d)   quarterly
    e)   bi-annually
    f)   annually

Answer the following questions by circling True or False.

1. True / False   Parents know what their children are learning each week in church.

2. True / False   Our church provides specific parenting resources to help parents stay actively involved in their child's spiritual development.

3. True / False   Parents know what their biblical responsibility is in their home.

4. True / False   We encourage children and teenagers to discuss spiritual matters with their parents.

5. True / False   Parents are the primary influencer in a child's life.

6. True / False   Most of our parents have a plan for the spiritual development of their children.

7. True / False   Pastors should equip parents to disciple their children.

8. True / False   Our church has a strategy to equip parents to disciple their children.

9. True / False   Our church evaluates how involved our parents are in their child's spiritual development.

10. True / False   Our church offers a parenting class every
                          year.

Please write your answers in the space provided.

1. Do you believe your church does a good job of equipping
    parents? Please explain your answer. _____
    _____
    _____
    _____
    _____
    _____

2. What is your church's strategy for helping parents take an
    active role in their child's spiritual development? Please explain
    your answer. _____
    _____
    _____
    _____
    _____
    _____

3. What is your church's greatest struggle as you think about
    equipping parents to disciple their children? Please explain
    your answer. _____
    _____
    _____
    _____
    _____
    _____

4. What steps can be taken to make equipping parents a priority
    in the life of your church? Please explain your answer. _____
    _____
    _____
    _____
    _____
    _____

Also in the
Participatory Study Series

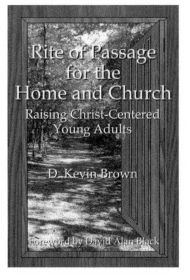

ROP was the perfect prod for me to enter young adulthood and most importantly, a closer walk with Jesus.
Katy - ROP Participant

Clear, concise, engaging, and oozing with heavenly wisdom ….

Dr. Jason Evans
Pastor/Elder,
Bethel Hill Baptist Church

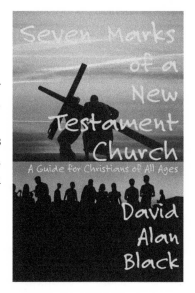

More from Energion Publications

Personal Study
Holy Smoke! Unholy Fire	Bob McKibben	$14.99
The Jesus Paradigm	David Alan Black	$17.99
When People Speak for God	Henry Neufeld	$17.99
The Sacred Journey	Chris Surber	$11.99

Christian Living
Faith in the Public Square	Robert D. Cornwall	$16.99
Grief: Finding the Candle of Light	Jody Neufeld	$8.99
Crossing the Street	Robert LaRochelle	$16.99

Bible Study
Learning and Living Scripture	Lentz/Neufeld	$12.99
From Inspiration to Understanding	Edward W. H. Vick	$24.99
Luke: A Participatory Study Guide	Geoffrey Lentz	$8.99
Philippians: A Participatory Study Guide	Bruce Epperly	$9.99
Ephesians: A Participatory Study Guide	Robert D. Cornwall	$9.99

Theology
Creation in Scripture	Herold Weiss	$12.99
Creation: the Christian Doctrine	Edward W. H. Vick	$12.99
The Politics of Witness	Allan R. Bevere	$9.99
Ultimate Allegiance	Robert D. Cornwall	$9.99
History and Christian Faith	Edward W. H. Vick	$9.99
The Church Under the Cross	William Powell Tuck	$11.99
The Journey to the Undiscovered Country	William Powell Tuck	$9.99
Eschatology: A Participatory Study Guide	Edward W. H. Vick	$9.99

Ministry
Clergy Table Talk	Kent Ira Groff	$9.99
Out of This World	Darren McClellan	$24.99
Wind and Whirlwind	David Moffett-Moore	$9.99

Generous Quantity Discounts Available
Dealer Inquiries Welcome
Energion Publications — P.O. Box 841
Gonzalez, FL_ 32560
Website: http://energionpubs.com
Phone: (850) 525-3916